THE PREHISTORIC PEOPLES
OF SCOTLAND

Studies in Ancient History and Archaeology

Editor: F. T. Wainwright

THE PREHISTORIC
PEOPLES
OF SCOTLAND

edited by

STUART PIGGOTT

Routledge and Kegan Paul

LONDON

First published 1962
by Routledge & Kegan Paul Limited
Broadway House, 68–74 Carter Lane
London, E.C.4

Printed in Great Britain
by W. & J. Mackay & Co. Ltd, Chatham

Contents

Illustrations

ILLUSTRATIONS

ACKNOWLEDGEMENTS

Plates 1, 2, 3, 7 and 8 are from photographs by Mr. Malcolm Murray, Department of Archaeology, University of Edinburgh; nos. 5 and 6 (left) by the National Museum of Antiquities, Edinburgh; no. 4 (*a*) by the Central Office of Information, and no. 4 (*b*) by the Ministry of Works.

Preface

THE chapters constituting this volume originated as a series of lectures given to the Scottish Summer School in Archaeology at its Edinburgh meeting in 1955. On the death of the School's organizer, Dr. F. T. Wainwright, I have taken over the editing of this volume, and while of necessity the long interval between the original construction of the contributions, and their appearance in print, has led to changed viewpoints and an accession of new material, so far as possible the necessary adjustments have been made.

STUART PIGGOTT

The University of Edinburgh
1962

CHAPTER ONE

Fishermen and Farmers

IT is a sobering thought, and one conducive to a proper sense of historical perspective, that before the first savages set foot upon the soil of Scotland the first urban, and in that sense civilized, community had been flourishing at Jericho for more than a thousand years.

The evidence for the earliest colonization of Scotland by man has been exhaustively examined by Lacaille,[1] whose conclusions accordingly need only a brief discussion here. In common with other workers, he distinguishes four main groups of pre-neolithic communities, each identified by its own characteristic stone and flint industry, and each referable to some part of the later stages of the Post-Glacial period. In terms of climatic and vegetational history, these mesolithic communities of hunter-fishers belong to the final stages of the Boreal and to the ensuing Atlantic phase; or in terms of the absolute chronology now being established, even if still only in skeletal form, by radio-carbon determinations, to the period from about 5500 B.C. to 3000 B.C.

The principal evidence upon which these signs of early occupation have been dated is their relationship to the 'raised beach' deposits laid down around the coasts of Scotland at a time when the mean sea-level stood some twenty-five to thirty feet higher than it does today, and the present littoral was consequently submerged. This submergence appears to have begun about the time of the Boreal-Atlantic transition, around 5000 B.C., and to have reached its maximum during the fourth millennium.

[1] A. D. Lacaille, *The Stone Age in Scotland*, 1954.

1

Thereafter the sea-level gradually dropped, and it is likely that the shore-lines were still receding seawards when the first neolithic colonists arrived during the third millennium B.C.[1]

The earliest mesolithic community hitherto identified is that represented by the Early Larnian flint assemblage recovered from the Post-Glacial raised beach on both sides of the North Channel. The incorporation of these worked flints *in* the beach deposits shows that they must be the remains of littoral settlements which flourished at an early stage of the coastal submergence and were subsequently overwhelmed by the rising sea. The original deposition of this material can thus be dated not much earlier than the end of the sixth millennium B.C.

The Larnian flint industry is characterized by the predominance of flakes and blades, and by the marked absence of microlithic elements. Generically at least it resembles the final stages of the Creswellian industry of the British Upper Palaeolithic; and it has in consequence been supposed to represent the results of a north-westerly migration of palaeolithic hunters, in Late Glacial or Early Post-Glacial times, from their former habitats in northern England, and their subsequent adoption of a strand-looping existence on the shores of the North Channel and the Clyde and Solway Firths.

By contrast, the microlithic industries differ very markedly from the Larnian both in distribution and in content. They occur notably in the valleys of the Clyde and Tweed (between which the Biggar Gap provided an easy route across the intervening watershed) and on Deeside in the neighbourhood of Banchory.[2] All the known material consists of surface finds, and no deposit has so far been discovered which can be securely dated by pollen analysis or other means. The resemblance between the Scottish material, however, and the microlithic industries of northern England[3] suggests that both are of much the same date. The Scottish sites, therefore, should represent settlement of the main river basins of the east and south of the country in Atlantic times (that is, during the fifth and fourth millennia B.C.), presumably by wandering bands of hunters moving gradually northwards up the eastern coastal plain of Durham and Northumberland to the Tweed, and spreading thence westwards to the Clyde by way of the Biggar Gap.

There remain two groups of mesolithic sites to be considered, both of

[1] Lacaille, *op. cit.*, 71–75.   [2] Lacaille, *op. cit.*, 161–7, 178–93.
[3] *Proc. Prehist. Soc.*, XXI (1955), 3–20.

2

which represent specialized forms of gathering and hunting economy closely tied, like that of the Larnians, to the sea-shore. In the valleys of the Forth and Tay, at a level corresponding to the high-water mark of the ancient Post-Glacial sea, traces of occupation have been found in the form of large heaps of the shells of edible molluscs;[1] while in the carse clays of the former estuary of the Forth, deposited during the marine transgression of Atlantic times, numerous finds have been made of the skeletons of stranded whales.[1] In four instances blubber-mattocks of red-deer antler, perforated to take a wooden handle, were found in association with the skeleton; and there is every reason to suppose that these tools belonged to the same families of strand-loopers who accumulated the shell-mounds on the shore. The monotony of the molluscan diet which these mounds represent doubtless ensured that the fortuitous arrival of a supply of several tons of red meat was eagerly awaited, and exploited with relish and dispatch.

The Obanian cave-settlements and shell-mounds on the coast of Argyll provide evidence for a comparable adaptation to sea-shore life, in a somewhat harsher environment. The remains of the tools of these strand-loopers are restricted in type and poor in quality. The most characteristic stone forms are fingerlike pebbles, generally worn or ground at one end to a blunt chisel-edge, to which the name 'limpet-scoop' has long been attached, presumably on the supposition that they were used for extracting uncooked limpets from their shells (for the extraction of *cooked* limpets no tool is required beyond the finger, or at the most another limpet-shell). Experiment readily shows, however, that while the removal of live limpets from their shells with these tools is extremely difficult, they are ideally fashioned for use as punches for detaching the limpet from the rock, using another pebble, or a piece of driftwood, as a hammer.

The associated flint industry is exceedingly poor and scanty, and consists of little more than utilized flakes. It is in bone and antler that the craftsmanship of the Obanians shows itself best; though even these materials are crudely worked by comparison with the sophisticated products of other mesolithic communities. The principal types are broad bone splinters, ground to a smooth blunt edge at one end, and somewhat resembling the limpet-punches, though doubtless used for some other purpose; and fish-spears with a double row of barbs, made from red-deer antler as well as from bone.

[1] Lacaille, *op. cit.*, 167–9, 175–8.

It is these spears which have been regarded as the type-fossil of the Obanian culture, and have in the past been compared significantly to similar weapons in the epipalaeolithic Azilian culture of south-western France.[1] But it has also been remarked that the Obanian tool-kit contains perforated antler mattocks precisely similar both to those found with whale-skeletons in the Forth Valley and, further afield, to examples from the Ertebølle 'Kitchen-midden' culture of Denmark. Since the presence of these Baltic elements in the Obanian has been recognized (initially by Mr. P. R. Ritchie, while working on the unpublished Obanian material in the Hunterian Museum), there has been a tendency to discount the earlier suggestion of an Atlantic origin for the culture in the French Azilian, and to regard it rather as a peripheral outpost of the later Forest Cultures of northern Europe. This tendency has also been encouraged by the obvious discrepancy in date between the Azilian and the Obanian. In the sequence of cultures the former follows immediately upon the final stages of the Upper Palaeolithic, and is hardly likely much to outlast the Late Glacial period, which ended around 8000 B.C. The Obanian sites, on the other hand, are later than the maximum transgression of the Post-Glacial sea, and cannot have been occupied much before 4000 B.C. The intervening gap of some four thousand years is obviously difficult to bridge, particularly since Azilian material has not so far been recorded on the Atlantic coasts elsewhere, either in north-western France or in Wales or western England.

Recently, however, Clark has suggested that the objections to an Azilian origin are not as cogent as they might seem.[2] The gap in geographical distribution is not necessarily significant, in view of the known mobility of communities based on hunting, fishing, and gathering; and in this particular case the absence of intermediate links in the chain may be more apparent than real, since the mesolithic coasts of France and south-western Britain are no longer available for study, having been submerged by the sea at some time since the middle of the second millennium B.C. The existence of megalithic and other stone structures now partially or wholly beneath the waves in Scilly and Brittany is well known.

The chronological discrepancy is also diminished if, as Clark suggests, the Obanian is regarded as a late and peripheral variant of the Larnian,[3]

[1] *Antiquity*, XXI (1947), 84–104.
[2] *Proc. Soc. Ant. Scot.*, LXXXIX (1955–56), 91–106.
[3] *Journ. Roy. Soc. Ant. Ireland*, LXXIX (1949), 170–81.

with perhaps the addition of Baltic Forest Culture elements which had been carried meanwhile across the Midland Valley by the expansion of similar strand-looping communities already established in the Forth and Tay estuaries. It is not impossible, however, that such Baltic influences might be discernible in the Larnian itself, had we any sites in which the bone and antler work of this culture was adequately represented.

In any case, the palaeobotanical evidence from the Early Larnian site at Toome on the shores of Lough Neagh in Northern Ireland [1] shows that the culture was already established in the area before the seventh millennium B.C., a date not very far removed from the *floruit* of the Azilian culture proper.

The adoption of this view of the origin of the Larnian and Obanian cultures necessarily requires also that we abandon the idea of deriving the former from the final Upper Palaeolithic communities of northern England. As Clark has pointed out, the Late Creswellian has been rather overworked as a suggested source for the non-microlithic aspects of the mesolithic cultures of Britain and, indeed, of the Continent;[2] and these doubts have now been significantly reinforced by a new and as yet unpublished discovery. During 1959 blasting operations near Kilmelfort in Argyll exposed the inner end of an inhabited cave containing the remains of an occupation-layer with an associated flint industry, a selection from which was exhibited by the excavator, Dr. John Coles, to the Spring Conference of the Prehistoric Society in 1960. It is clear that this industry resembles the later stages of the Creswellian very much more closely than does any aspect of the Larnian. This discovery thus goes some way to confirm the suggestion of a north-westerly migration of Creswellian people to the west coasts of Scotland. But it also makes it the less probable that the origin of the Larnian culture is to be sought in such a migration, and to this extent the alternative of an Azilian origin is rendered all the more acceptable.

Questions of origin apart, however, it is clear that the territories of the earliest mesolithic colonists were not confined wholly to the west coasts, for from Kingsteps Quarry, near Nairn, there is evidence for human settlement as early, probably, as the fifth millennium B.C. Here a very crude series of worked tools in quartz, chert, and sandstone has been recovered from a thin layer of peat resting on, and covered by, blown sand, which

[1] Lacaille, *op. cit.*, 124.
[2] *Proc. Soc. Ant. Scot.*, LXXXIX (1955–56), 102.

has been shown to have formed during the Boreal-Atlantic transition (*circa* 5000 B.C.) and afterwards.[1] The precise level or levels in the peat from which the artefacts came is not recorded; but the crudity of the workmanship and the absence of any specific microlithic forms argues for an early date, before the penetration of north-eastern Scotland by true microlithic cultures. The presence of oak charcoal in association with a microlithic industry at Birkwood on Deeside[2] suggests that this penetration did not take place before the Atlantic period, as might indeed be expected from evidence elsewhere.

The number of individual sites of the mesolithic period now known in Scotland numbers at least one hundred; but it should not be assumed that these represent more than an exceedingly small population. Many of these sites are marked only by a scatter of flints, which may be no more than the product of a few hours' activity by a single flint-knapper, or at best the debris of a temporary camping-site, occupied for a few days by a small band of roving hunters, and then abandoned. Such is the speed at which a skilled flint-knapper works, and such the quantity of waste flint produced in a very short time, that the wanderings of a single family could account, in the space of no more than a few years, for all the finds of microlithic flints in the whole of southern Scotland.

Nor should it be supposed that the very bulky accumulations of food-waste on coastal sites must represent communities larger than a single family, or settlement of long duration. It has been suggested, for instance, that a shell-mound measuring 100 by 60 feet, and from 1 to 3 feet in thickness, 'points to a fairly long occupation'.[3] But it must not be forgotten that of all forms of food, shell-fish produce the greatest bulk of refuse for a given quantity of edible substance. It is thus by no means difficult, where limpets, whelks, mussels, oysters, winkles or cockles form a substantial part of the diet, for the waste shells to accumulate at least at the rate of a large bucketful, or half a cubic foot, per head per day. A group of ten people could thus amass a midden of the size quoted in less than seven years of continuous settlement, or within a single lifetime of seasonal camping on the sea-shore.

All the evidence suggests, therefore, that the mesolithic population of Scotland was exceedingly sparse. By way of comparison, it may be noted

[1] *Trans. Botanical Soc. Edinburgh*, XXXVI (1954), 224–9.
[2] *Proc. Soc. Ant. Scot.*, LXX (1935–36), 421.
[3] Lacaille, *op. cit.*, 176.

that for Denmark, where a single large bog can contain up to a hundred separate settlement sites, the total mesolithic population has been estimated at no more than 125 persons. The area of Scotland is about twice that of Denmark; but when the mountainous regions, unsuitable for colonization even by hunter-fishers, are subtracted the *habitable* areas of the two countries are about the same. In view of the far smaller number of sites of the period known in Scotland, one is forced to the conclusion that until the neolithic colonization the population at any one time can hardly have exceeded two people for each of the modern counties.

The groups of neolithic colonists who arrived during the third millennium B.C. must therefore be regarded as the earliest settlers to have reached Scotland in any substantial numbers. They would be confronted with a terrain hitherto virtually uninhabited, and certainly unchanged by man from its natural condition; and it is thus improbable that the pattern of neolithic settlement was in any way influenced or controlled by the minute population of native savages.

The cultural identity of the first neolithic settlers in Scotland is not at present entirely certain. It has long been recognized that among the 'Primary Neolithic' communities of Britain two principal and separate elements can be distinguished: on the one hand the 'Windmill Hill' or 'Western Neolithic' culture, characterized by various forms of pottery and by the collective inhumation of the dead beneath unchambered earthen long barrows, and concentrated principally in the Lowland Zone of England; and on the other hand the builders of gallery graves, covered by elongated stone cairns, centred respectively upon the Bristol Channel and the North Channel between Scotland and Ireland.

In the past it has been assumed almost without question that it was the latter group, the builders of long cairns or gallery graves, who were alone responsible for the introduction of the neolithic economy to the northern kingdom.[1] But in the course of time a growing body of evidence has accumulated for primary neolithic settlement in Scotland which is neither physically associated with chambered tombs, nor conforms in its geographical pattern to their predominantly western and northern distribution. The whole question of the settlement of Scotland by the earliest farmers thus requires examination.

The problem of origins has, moreover, been further complicated in recent years by the recognition that the so-called Windmill Hill culture of

[1] V. G. Childe, *The Prehistory of Scotland* (1935), 22–79.

England comprises diverse elements which in all probability should be derived from widely separated areas of continental Europe; and that so far from being merely the British representative of the 'Western' family of Atlantic neolithic cultures, it includes also 'Eastern' elements related to the Funnel-Beaker and Michelsberg cultures of the North European plain and the Low Countries.[1]

Some degree of duality and diversity within the Windmill Hill culture has indeed long been implicit in the restricted distribution of unchambered earthen long barrows, which are largely confined to the chalk areas of eastern and southern England and do not occur at all in western districts, even where pottery types of specifically western and Atlantic origin are known. This geographical pattern can hardly be explained merely in geological terms, since there is no reason why *unchambered* long barrows should not have been built in any district. The differences between the chambered tombs of the west and the unchambered long barrows of the south and east must be accounted for not by the mere presence or absence of suitable building stone, but as the respective expressions of two distinct and divergent traditions of collective inhumation: in the first, of successive burial in a tomb chamber to which repeated access could be had; and in the second of the simultaneous burial of a number of bodies (or skeletons) collected and stored elsewhere in the period preceding the building of the barrow. In other words, we are dealing with a cultural distinction between family vaults and mass graves.

The full implications of the internal complexity of the Windmill Hill culture, loosely so called, have still to be worked out in detail. In fig. 1, however, an attempt has been made to differentiate at least part of the basic pattern of 'eastern' and 'western' elements, by means of selected and apparently diagnostic types of pottery. The forms chosen to represent the western element are plain lugged bowls of Piggott's shapes A, B and C,[2] whose origins in the Early Chassey culture of France are perhaps hardly in doubt. Only lugged examples of these forms have been plotted, since plain bag-shaped pots *without* lugs are so simple and basic a form that they are unlikely in themselves to have much cultural significance.

To represent the eastern element I have chosen the graceful shouldered bowls of Piggott's shape G, in which the neck above the shoulder is distinctly concave, and thus to be distinguished from superficially similar

---

[1] *Proc. Prehist. Soc.*, XXI (1955), 96–101.
[2] *Arch. Journ.*, LXXXVIII (1931), 75.

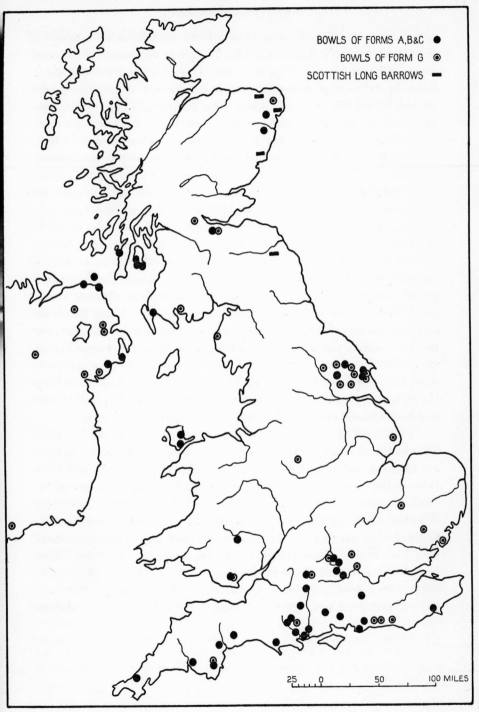

25   0   50   100 MILES

Fig. 1. Neolithic pottery types and Scottish long barrows.

carinated or shouldered forms in which the neck is either conical or cylindrical (Piggott's shapes D and E). Though in the past there has been some confusion between Piggott's forms D and G, an attempt is made below (p. 14) to show that they are culturally as well as morphologically distinct. The bowls of form G, which alone are plotted in fig. 1, were long ago compared with the Michelsberg 'tulip-beakers' of Belgium,[1] and there seems no reason now against returning to this view of their origin. Admittedly it was at one time abandoned on the ground that the Michelsberg culture of the Rhineland was chronologically too late to have stood in any prototypical relationship to our own Windmill Hill culture;[2] and indeed the latest study of the Michelsberg groups on the Continent suggests that in Belgium at least the analogues of our form G bowls appear after rather than before 2000 B.C.[3] Once it is accepted, however, that the Windmill Hill culture of Britain is a cultural amalgam of diverse elements, it is no longer necessary, or even wise, to assume that its various components reached these islands simultaneously from different directions. There is thus no inherent difficulty in positing a North European origin for our form G bowls, provided that it is recognized at the same time that their arrival was subsequent to that of the 'western' components of the culture. The purpose of fig. 1, however, is not to illustrate a discussion of the origins of the Windmill Hill culture, but to show that within the culture itself a differentiation into regional elements is possible, and that both regional elements here distinguished extend into Scotland.

The pattern of these two contrasted types shows that the 'western' material has two main areas of concentration, in southern and south-western England, and around the North Channel, respectively, the two areas being linked by a few finds in South Wales and Anglesey. Elsewhere in the north the distribution is eastern, in Yorkshire, West Lothian, and Aberdeenshire. It is perhaps significant that in the western area outside England more than half the sites from which these lugged types of pottery have been recovered are chambered tombs, belonging or related to the Severn-Cotswold and Clyde-Carlingford series (Ty Isaf, Tinkinswood, Bryn yr Hen Bobl, and Pant y Saer in Wales; Audleystown in Northern Ireland; and Beacharra, Clachaig, Torlin, and Sliddery Water in western

[1] *Proc. Prehist. Soc. East Anglia*, VII (1934), 379.

[2] S. Piggott, *Neolithic Cultures of the British Isles* (1954), 74.

[3] *Proc. Prehist. Soc.*, XXV (1959), 51–134. The new 'long' chronology for the neolithic imposed by radio-carbon dates makes it difficult now to accept so low a *terminus post quem*.

Scotland). The remaining occurrences in the North Channel area are all on sand-dune or other coastal sites.

It has already been suggested that some generic relationship must exist between the Severn-Cotswold and the Clyde-Carlingford series of gallery graves;[1] and this suggestion is confirmed in a specific sense by Dr. Daniel in the succeeding chapter (p. 66), where the problems posed by the megalithic tombs of Scotland are discussed in detail. It is enough here to point out that the distribution of these 'western' forms of pottery reinforces the conclusions to be drawn from the morphology of the tombs themselves, namely that the initial colonization of south-western Scotland is likely to have had its proximal origin in the Bristol Channel area. It must be admitted, of course, that these forms of lugged 'western' pottery are not particularly well represented in the Severn-Cotswold tombs themselves, and indeed so far have not been recorded at all from the North Wiltshire group of tombs, whose semicircular forecourts most closely resemble those of the Clyde-Carlingford series. It is thus possible, though by no means necessary, to suggest that the pottery and the tombs respectively mark the course of two parallel but distinct movements of colonization of the same northern area from the same southern source.

What does seem almost certain, however, is that this movement up the Irish Sea, whether simple in character or complex, resulted in the earliest settlement of any part of Scotland by groups practising the neolithic farming economy. The date of this initial colonization is still obscure; but in view of the general lengthening of neolithic chronologies in Europe as a whole required by recent radio-carbon dates (none of which are yet available for Scottish sites), it is likely to have been before rather than after 2000 B.C.

This view of the identity of the earliest colonists is thus no more than a repetition of the conclusion reached by Childe a quarter of a century ago. It is rather for the later stages of neolithic settlement, and particularly of the eastern districts of the country hardly penetrated by the builders of chambered tombs, that new interpretations of the evidence are now possible. Here, it appears, two separate movements of neolithic immigration can be detected: the first, at scattered points up the east coast as far as Aberdeenshire, marking a northwards extension of the 'eastern' elements in the Windmill Hill culture of the south; and the second, terminating in the same region but originating ultimately in the Lyles Hill culture of Northern Ireland.

[1] Piggott, *Neolithic Cultures* (1954), 182.

11

The evidence for the first of these movements, so far as pottery is concerned, is scanty. Fragments of bowls of form G have been recovered from the three sites shown in fig. 1 (Cairnpapple, West Lothian; Bantaskine, near Stirling; and Powsode Cairn on Atherb Farm in Buchan). The second of these is a particularly fine and well-made shouldered bowl which closely resembles vessels from Yorkshire.

Were this the only evidence, one could hardly speak with any confidence of a separate movement of colonists up the east coasts from Yorkshire, particularly as pottery of this form also occurs in Ulster (fig. 1), where it apparently represents a secondary colonization from Yorkshire by way of the Solway Firth. It would thus be possible to explain these isolated occurrences of bowls of form G in Scotland as one result of the immigration from Ulster discussed below.

That this view of their origin is the less probable, however, is suggested by the presence in eastern Scotland of four long barrows (fig. 1), the characteristic burial-mound of the Windmill Hill culture in southern and eastern England. The most southerly of the Scottish examples, at Caverton Hillhead, south of Kelso, has long since been entirely destroyed, but is reliably recorded to have consisted 'of fine loose mould, intermixed with large stones, covered over with heath'. It measured 340 feet in length, the width tapering from about 40 feet at the eastern end to 30 at the western.[1] This can hardly have been anything but a long barrow.

The second site, on a hill-top overlooking the sea above Gourdon, Kincardineshire, has again been shown, by probing with a steel bar, to be composed mainly of earth, with only occasional stones. It is orientated roughly N.E.–S.W., with a length of 155 feet and a height of 9 feet, the width tapering from 40 to 25 feet, the broader end lying to the N.E.[2] There is no apparent ditch.

The third site has not previously been published. It lies on a small hillock, now planted with oak trees, about half a mile S.S.E. of Pitlurg Station in the parish of Slains, Aberdeenshire, and about 3 miles N.E. of the head of the estuary of the River Ythan. The mound is of earth, containing no stones detectable with a probe, and is orientated 7° W. of true north. It is about 70 feet in length and 5 feet in height, and tapers fairly sharply to the south from a maximum width of 25 feet. The mound appears to stand on a sloping berm or platform about 15 feet wide on each

[1] Roy. Comm. Anc. Mon. Scotland, *Roxburghshire Inventory* (1956), 133, no. 218.
[2] *Proc. Soc. Ant. Scot.*, LVIII (1923–24), 23–24.

side, at the base of which in places there are suggestions of a silted ditch; but this may be an optical illusion due to the presence of a modern raised bank surrounding the plantation. There are no signs of previous excavation.

The last of these Scottish long barrows stands, like the Gourdon example, in a commanding position on a hill-top overlooking the sea. It is locally known as the Longman Cairn, and lies near the coast of Banffshire about $2\frac{1}{2}$ miles E.S.E. of Macduff. Its overall length is 220 feet, with an orientation 30° E. of N. The northern end is about 14 feet high and is divided from the remainder by a transverse hollow, possibly the site of an unrecorded excavation. The width of the main mound tapers from 40 to 25 feet, with a height of about 9 feet throughout the greater part of its length. Modern quarrying into the side of the mound shows it to be built mainly of earth, and probing detected relatively few stones.[1]

While admittedly none of these sites would be entirely at home among the long barrows of southern England, it is none the less difficult to assume that they are merely earthen versions of long megalithic cairns, since true long cairns, built wholly of stones, do occur in the same regions. In the south-east there are the Mutiny Stones in Berwickshire[2] and the Kirshope Cairn in Roxburghshire;[3] while Aberdeenshire contains at least three similar sites, at Cloghill, west of Aberdeen,[4] at Balnagowan near Aboyne,[5] and at Knapperty Hillock, near Auchmachar in Buchan.[6] It seems far more satisfactory to accept these four sites for what they appear to be, namely earthen long barrows of Windmill Hill type, and to relate them to the sporadic occurrences of pottery of form G which is appropriate to the same culture.

It is thus possible to envisage two divergent movements in the northwards spread of the Windmill Hill culture, both originating in Yorkshire. The first took a north-westerly route to the shores of the Solway Firth, and thence to Ulster; while the second continued northwards up the east coast. Finds of plain undifferentiated Windmill Hill pottery at Old Bewick, Northumberland, on the Gullane Sands in East Lothian, and at Roslin, near Edinburgh, help to fill out the meagre evidence for this northward

[1] *Proc. Soc. Ant. Scot.*, LIX (1924–25), 21–28.
[2] *Proc. Soc. Ant. Scot.*, LIX (1924–25), 198–204.
[3] Roy. Comm. Anc. Mon. Scotland, *Roxburghshire Inventory* (1956), 94, no. 110.
[4] *Proc. Soc. Ant. Scot.*, LIX (1924–25), 21–22.
[5] *Proc. Soc. Ant. Scot.*, LIX (1924–25), 26.
[6] *Proc. Soc. Ant. Scot.*, XXXVIII (1903–04), 273.

penetration; but even so the pattern is sufficiently discontinuous to suggest movement principally by sea. It is noteworthy that all the sites where the relevant pottery or long barrows occur are within easy reach either of the sea itself or of major river valleys.

The probability of this northwards extension of the Windmill Hill culture has been recognized in the past, and indeed its farthest limit has been carried beyond the Buchan region to the coast of the Moray Firth, to include the well-known finds of pottery from Easterton of Roseisle near Burghead.[1] It seems more likely, however, that this and the other finds of related forms of pottery from Scotland shown in fig. 2 originated not in the Windmill Hill culture of the south and east, but in the Lyles Hill culture of Northern Ireland.

The diagnostic forms and decoration of Lyles Hill pottery used here are well illustrated at the type-site.[2] They consist of shouldered bowls of Piggott's forms D and E, in which the neck above the shoulder (itself often of ledge or stepped form) is respectively conical or approximately cylindrical. Both these forms should be distinguished from the bowls of form G already discussed, in which the neck has the form of a trumpet-mouth, with a concave flare. The rims of Lyles Hill ware are frequently bent outwards sharply, and sometimes expanded internally as well, in contrast to the plain or beaded rims of the form G bowls. The commonest form of ornament is a highly characteristic 'finger-tip fluting' of the surface, usually on the exterior or flattened rim only, but occasionally inside the neck as well.

The area shown in fig. 2 includes the majority of sites on which pottery of this type is known.[3] Elsewhere there are only scattered occurrences in central and southern Ireland, the Isle of Man, west Wales and south-west England. In the northern part of the Windmill Hill province in England these characteristic shapes of pottery are unknown; and though finger-tip fluting has been recorded occasionally on Heslerton ware in Yorkshire, it is there confined entirely to the rims of pots, and may perhaps be accounted for by influence from Northern Ireland, a reflex of the movement which carried the form G bowls from Yorkshire to Ulster.

In Northern Ireland itself, Lyles Hill ware occurs fairly frequently in

[1] Piggott, *Neolithic Cultures* (1954), 271–2.

[2] E. Estyn Evans, *Lyles Hill* (1953), 32–43.

[3] The map was prepared some time before the appearance of H. J. Case's study of Irish Neolithic pottery (*Proc. Prehist. Soc.*, XXVII (1961), 174–233). The term 'Lyles Hill' is used here in a less specific sense.

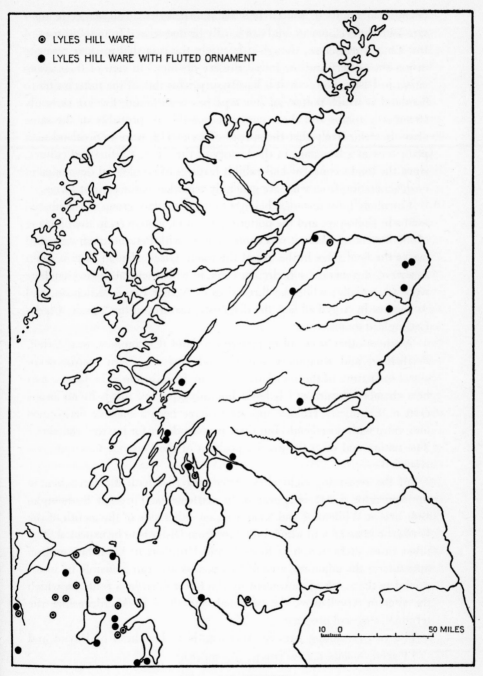

Fig. 2. Lyles Hill Ware.

chambered tombs of the Clyde-Carlingford series at all stages in their typological development, and can hardly be dissociated from the spread of the tombs themselves; though it is surely the case that in their ultimate origin the pottery and the burial rite are distinct.[1] In view of their association in Ulster, however, it is hardly surprising that of the sixteen sites in Scotland at which pottery of this type has been found, five are certainly chambered tombs and three more are possibly or probably of the same class. It seems likely that the spread of Lyles Hill ware to Scotland took place only at a late stage in the history of the Clyde-Carlingford culture, since the tombs concerned all exhibit features of typological development or degeneration from what are generally regarded as the earliest forms.

Cairnholy I, for instance, belongs to the secondary group of chambered tombs in Galloway; and the pottery was found, moreover, in the blocking of the forecourt, where it was contemporary with Peterborough ware and marks the final stage in the use of the tomb. Glecknabae in Bute is again a cairn of 'degenerate' sub-circular form, in which several single chambers were set radially; while the three sites of Nether Largie, Kilchoan, and Achnacree in Argyll all lack the diagnostic features of the 'classic' Clyde-Carlingford tombs.

At three other sites, all in eastern Scotland (Cultoquhey, near Crieff, Perthshire; and Knapperty Hillock and Powsode Cairn in Aberdeenshire) the nature of the associated structure is uncertain. The former *may* be a chambered cairn of Clyde-Carlingford type, but this is by no means certain. Knapperty Hillock appears to have been a massive flat-topped long cairn with raised ends, but there is no evidence for internal chambers. The nature and even the precise position of the Powsode Cairn are unrecorded.

Of the remaining eight sites (listed, together with the foregoing, in the Appendix, p. 34) six appear to be settlements. Three, at Rothesay in Bute and at Whitemoss and Knappers, on either side of the mouth of the Clyde, lie in an area in which influence from Ulster is to be expected. The other three, at Easterton of Roseisle and Urquhart in Elginshire and on Speyside in the adjoining area of Inverness-shire, can plausibly be interpreted as the result of movement up the Great Glen by a route on which the sites in Argyll mark the proximal, and those in Aberdeenshire the terminal, stages of progress.

The two remaining sites in Aberdeenshire, Loanhead of Daviot and

[1] Piggott, *Neolithic Cultures* (1954), 167–70, 182.

East Finnercy, require more detailed comment. The Recumbent Stone Circle at the former site is well known; but the existence among the pottery from the site of a few sherds of Lyles Hill ware has only recently been recognized.[1] The interpretation and dating of these enigmatic monuments of north-eastern Scotland is admittedly still obscure; but the discovery of Beaker sherds at Loanhead of Daviot itself and at Old Keig,[2] and of a fragmentary polished stone bracer of Beaker type, associated with sherds 'of a reddish colour' at Old Rayne,[3] make it overwhelmingly probable that this form of sepulchral cairn was current during the Beaker occupation of Aberdeenshire, with which at least some of the local Lyles Hill ware must be contemporary, as is shown by the finds from the East Finnercy cairn discussed below.

In spite of the occurrence of Beaker sherds in three of the Recumbent Stone Circles (and very few more than this have been even partially excavated by modern techniques), it is difficult to regard them primarily as Beaker monuments, since such structures are unknown in the continental homeland of the Beaker peoples. It is surely more satisfactory to see the occurrence of these Beaker sherds as yet another illustration of the ability of the Beaker culture to adapt itself to indigenous institutions, an ability already well demonstrated by the frequent finds of Beaker pottery in megalithic tombs, and by the development within Britain of a specifically Beaker variant of the Secondary Neolithic form of henge monument.[4]

If the origin of the Recumbent Stone Circle is to be sought outside Aberdeenshire, it is perhaps not wholly fanciful to look to the type-site of the Lyles Hill Culture in Ulster, where the cairn on the hill-top exhibits many of the specific features of the Aberdeenshire sites, and was undoubtedly built by the makers of Lyles Hill pottery. The site consists of a low ring-cairn surrounding a central space containing a cremated burial, and bordered by a boulder kerb which is broken at one point by a miniature 'recumbent stone' set between a pair of 'flankers'.[5] These are all features which are repeated, though in more massive form, in the Recumbent Stone Circles proper. The only element clearly lacking at Lyles Hill is

---

[1] The recognition of this pottery is due to Miss Audrey Henshall, to whom the writer is most grateful for the information.

[2] *Proc. Soc. Ant. Scot.*, LXVII (1932–33), 45.

[3] *Proc. Soc. Ant. Scot.*, XXXVI (1901–02), 530.

[4] R. J. C. Atkinson, C. M. Piggott, and N. K. Sandars, *Excavations at Dorchester, Oxon.*, I (1951), 93.

[5] Evans, *Lyles Hill* (1953), 5.

the surrounding circle of free-standing uprights; but this may well be an accretion from native sources in Scotland, as it appears to be in the Clava passage graves and ring cairns.[1] In the absence of any more convincing evidence it may therefore be suggested, though with reserve, that the development of the Recumbent Stone Circle in Aberdeenshire is to be related to the colonization of the same area by representatives of the Lyles Hill culture of Ireland.

Supporting evidence for this colonization, and for its late date, comes from the round cairn at East Finnercy, Dunecht, about eleven miles W. of Aberdeen. Neolithic pottery, including lugged bowls, had been found during a casual excavation of the site in the 1920s;[2] and when the cairn was visited by Professor Piggott and the writer in 1951 a short section of dry stone walling was visible on the surface near the centre which, if original, suggested the presence of a passage grave. Accordingly the cairn was partially excavated by the writer in the summer of 1952.[3]

The dry stone walling proved to be a recent feature, built by the previous excavators to retain their dump, as was subsequently confirmed by one of them who visited the site. The whole of the centre of the cairn, which stood to a height of some 5 feet, had been disturbed. None of the stones found in the central area, however, were of a size or character to have served as the sides or capstone of a cist, nor were stone-holes for the base of a cist found in the old ground surface beneath the cairn. Moreover, our informant was certain that in the earlier opening no trace of a cist, or indeed of a burial of any kind, had been found.

On these grounds alone it was improbable that the site was a normal cairn of the Bronze Age; and this was confirmed by the quantity of sherds of neolithic pottery, almost all of Lyles Hill ware, and by a well-made leaf-shaped arrowhead of reddish Buchan flint, which occurred principally on the old surface beneath the cairn, and to a lesser extent in the soil filling the interstices beneath the stones. This neolithic material was confined to the cairn itself, and was not found even a short way outside its edge in the surrounding field. It is thus clear that the cairn was built by the makers of the pottery, and that this was deliberately deposited.

The pottery included a single sherd of cord-zoned Beaker, sealed beneath an undisturbed part of the cairn and only a few inches from

[1] *Proc. Soc. Ant. Scot.*, LXXXVIII (1954–55), 197.
[2] *Proc. Soc. Ant. Scot.*, LXIII (1928–29), 62–63.
[3] Report to be published in *Proceedings of the Society of Antiquaries of Scotland.*

fragments of Lyles Hill ware. There can be no doubt that here both types of pottery were strictly contemporary, and this association confirms the apparent association of the same types at Loanhead of Daviot. The Lyles Hill occupation of Aberdeenshire must thus overlap with at least the earlier stages of the Beaker colonization.

In view of the connexions between Ulster and Aberdeenshire already suggested above, it is significant that the best parallels for the East Finnercy cairn are to be found in several neolithic round cairns excavated in Northern Ireland, and notably that at Knockiveagh in Co. Down, in which the characteristic feature is the quantity of broken neolithic pottery and other debris of occupation deposited beneath or in the cairn.[1] The same practice also typifies the cairn on Lyles Hill itself.

The sherds with lug-handles found earlier at East Finnercy and at Loanhead of Daviot may possibly be connected with the movement from the Windmill Hill province up the east coast referred to above (p. 11). But it is perhaps better to regard them as an integral component of the Lyles Hill material from the same two sites, particularly as the examples from East Finnercy have lugs of the 'eared' or upward-pointing variety which seem to be particularly characteristic of Ireland.

One final piece of evidence for cultural links between Ulster and Aberdeenshire requires brief mention, namely the distribution in Scotland of stone axes of porcellanite from the axe factories of Tievebulliagh in Antrim and Rathlin Island off the Antrim coast.[2] Though a detailed picture of the occurrence of these axes in Scotland is not yet available, it is surely significant that outside the western coastal areas centred on the Clyde mouth, where their presence is readily to be understood, the principal concentration lies precisely in the north-east, in Aberdeenshire and the adjacent counties.[3]

The evidence discussed above for the neolithic settlement of eastern Scotland is too diverse, and numerically too scanty, to give any reliable picture of the relative density of population in different areas. On this point, however, it is instructive to examine the distribution of the commonest of all forms of neolithic artefact, the leaf-shaped flint arrowhead. The collections of the National Museum of Antiquities contain a very

[1] *Ulster Journ. Arch.*, XX (1957), 8–20.
[2] *Ulster Journ, Arch.*, XV (1952), 31–60.
[3] A map, including unpublished identifications, is exhibited in the Kelvingrove Museum, Glasgow.

large number of specimens of this type, and the results of a count by areas are given in fig. 3. It should be noted that the horizontal scale of the diagram expresses *relative* density per unit area of habitable land, on the assumption that the present distribution of arable cultivation is, by and

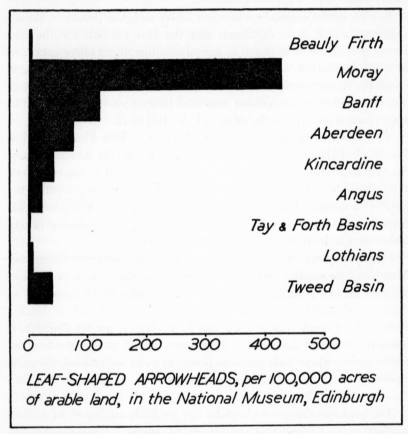

Fig. 3. Leaf-shaped arrowheads in Scotland.

large, a measure of the territory available for primary settlement by early agriculturalists. It is to be expected, of course, that arrowheads will be found over a wider area than that suitable for primitive tillage, since it is in the marginal areas that hunting is likely to have been most intensive.

It may be objected, of course, that the apparent distribution of artifacts of this kind reflects the relative density of modern flint-collectors rather than of prehistoric settlement; and it is certainly true in the present case that the exceptional density of finds in the county of Moray is due to the activities of collectors on a single site, the Culbin Sands, long known as a happy hunting ground. None the less, it is also true that collectors are most active and most successful precisely where flints themselves are most numerous; and to that extent the diagram may be put forward at least as a generalized picture of the relative density of primary neolithic settlement. It is at once apparent that the main concentration is in the north-east, and that the frequency falls progressively southwards to the Firth of Forth. In spite of the known fertility of the soil (and of the opportunities of discovery afforded by widespread arable cultivation) the Lothians, and particularly East Lothian, appear to have been only sparsely settled; and it is only in the Tweed basin that the density of occupation approaches that of the regions north of the Tay. The overall picture given by this kind of evidence thus reinforces the indications of the pottery and other material discussed above.

In summary, therefore, the primary neolithic colonization of Scotland can be separated into three phases of settlement, each represented by characteristic forms of pottery and of sites in the field. The first had its primary impact in the south-west, and cannot be separated from the introduction of megalithic gallery graves to the same region, probably well before 2000 B.C. The results of this impact, and of the arrival in Scotland of the builders of passage graves, are discussed fully in the following chapter. The second movement, originating probably in Yorkshire, carried aspects of the 'eastern' element in the Windmill Hill culture of England as far north as Buchan; while the third saw the implantation in the north-east of an offshoot of the regional neolithic culture of Ulster, probably by way of the Great Glen and the coast of the Moray Firth.

The initial dates of these two latter movements are at present difficult to determine. In southern England at least one unchambered long barrow, at Nutbane near Andover, appears to have been completed, at latest, soon after 2500 B.C. and perhaps several centuries earlier.[1] Yet the Skendleby long barrow in Lincolnshire must be contemporary with sherds of Cord-zoned Beaker pottery,[2] which even on the Continent can hardly be dated much earlier than 2200 B.C.[3] The introduction of earthen

[1] *Antiquity*, XXXIII (1959), 289.
[2] *Archaeologia*, LXXXV (1935), 53.
[3] *Antiquity*, XXXIV (1960), 17. The date there given requires the addition of approximately two centuries to correct it for the Suess effect.

long barrows into eastern Scotland may thus have taken place at any time during the last three-quarters of the third millennium B.C., though on geographical grounds a date towards the end of this period is the more probable.

The possible chronological limits for the expansion of the Lyles Hill culture are if anything even wider. The date of the Knockiveagh cairn in Ulster, already referred to (p. 19), probably lies in the range 3400–2700 B.C.;[1] whereas at East Finnercy the association with Cord-zoned Beaker pottery again gives an initial date of around 2200 B.C. at the earliest. The *minimum* distance in time between these two very similar sites must thus be of the order of half a millennium. If we are to accept the long chronology for the British Neolithic imposed by the radio-carbon dates, we must equally accept that the lives of individual cultures, and of individual types of construction, must be far longer than we have hitherto been willing to allow.

For both of these later movements the terminal area is Aberdeenshire and the adjacent counties. Whatever the factors that rendered this district particularly attractive to the earliest farmers, they must have operated with equal force upon the Secondary Neolithic population, now to be discussed, whose distribution shows a similar bias towards the north-east.

The concept of the Secondary Neolithic, as the result of the cultural and technological impact of Primary Neolithic agriculturalists and herdsmen upon surviving mesolithic groups of hunters and fishermen, is now well established and has been fruitfully applied outside as well as within Britain, where it was first evolved.[2] In the United Kingdom the basic diagnostic elements of these cultures include, first, specific forms of pottery, of the Peterborough, Rinyo-Clacton, and Sandhill types, each with a markedly regional distribution; secondly, tools and weapons in flint and stone, which both morphologically and geographically are more uniform than the pottery and reflect, in many instances, the persistence of mesolithic traditions in fashion and craftsmanship; and thirdly, ritual sites including embanked open-air sanctuaries, or henge-monuments, and individual or collective burials. The latter occur occasionally both in caves and in round barrows, and rarely as collective cremations associated with monuments of 'henge' type.

In Scotland the manifestations of Secondary Neolithic culture can be

[1] *Antiquity*, XXXIV (1960), 112.
[2] Piggott, *Neolithic Cultures* (1954), 276–301.

divided into two main groups. On the one hand there are those which are likely to have originated in England, where they are far better represented, and whose presence in the north can be explained by the migration of cultural groups already fully formed in the south; these are plotted in fig. 4. On the other hand, there are types which seem to be largely or wholly of native Scottish origin, of which the two leading forms, perforated maceheads and carved stone balls, are separately mapped.

Of the pottery types, Peterborough ware (fig. 4) occurs only on the few sites listed in the Appendix (p. 35), and on none of these is it represented by more than a few sherds. Apart from a doubtful example at Scotstarvit in Fife, it is restricted to the region south of the Clyde-Forth line, which accordingly marks the extreme northern frontier of a cultural group specifically adapted to the more genial climate and landscape of southern England.

Rinyo-Clacton ware has a much wider, though very discontinuous, distribution in Scotland, and one which on the west coast, at any rate, can hardly be interpreted except by a sea-borne movement. The origins of this form of pottery, outside Britain, have still satisfactorily to be determined. But in view of the generally accepted analogues for its decoration among the late neolithic Chassey II wares of western France,[1] and of the occurrence in passage graves in Orkney and Caithness of stone and bone types which accompany Rinyo-Clacton ware at the sites of Skara Brae and Rinyo, one may hazard the guess that the spread of this pottery up the west coasts to the far north is in some way to be connected with the spread of the passage graves themselves.

The great value of the excavations at the two principal sites of the Rinyo-Clacton culture in the north should not be allowed to obscure the fact that Skara Brae and Rinyo are *sui generis*, and cannot be taken as typical of Secondary Neolithic settlements even on the mainland of Scotland, let alone elsewhere in Britain. Structurally they represent a specific adaptation to the exigencies of a treeless environment, in which the only organic building materials were driftwood and the bones of whales, both of uncertain and fortuitous supply; while the finds from both sites, and particularly the bone and stone artifacts, show marked influences from the Circumpolar Stone Age cultures of the Sub-Arctic Zone, in a degree unparalleled in any other Rinyo-Clacton site farther to the south.

The remaining types which can be regarded as of ultimately southern

[1] Piggott, *Neolithic Cultures* (1954), 344–6.

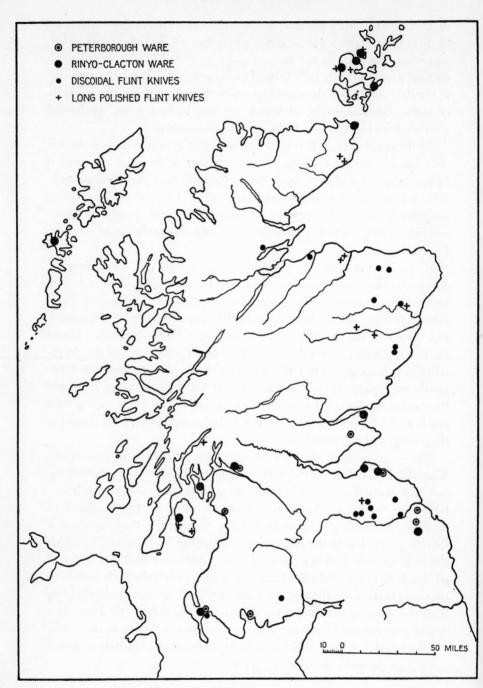

Fig. 4. Secondary Neolithic pottery and flint types

origin are flint knives with polished edges; jet 'sliders' or belt-fasteners; and perhaps flint arrowheads of the chisel-edged and lop-sided forms derived from the *petit-tranchet* type of the mesolithic Northern Forest cultures.

The distribution of two types of flint knives with polished edges is shown in fig. 4. The first is generally elongated, of blade-like form, often with only one long edge treated by grinding or polishing, but sometimes polished all over. Such knives occur in England in well-established Secondary Neolithic contexts, particularly with burials of the Dorchester culture.[1] The second is the discoidal knife, generally larger and sometimes more carefully finished than the former type. On grounds of distribution only (for no specimen has yet been found in unequivocal association) Clark ascribed these to the Beaker cultures.[2] But they are not known in Beaker contexts on the Continent, and their distribution accords equally well with that of other varieties of Secondary Neolithic material in Britain.

In Scotland both types occur predominantly in the east, but with some differences of local distribution. The long knives are found right up to the extreme north, in Caithness and Orkney, where in three instances they are associated with passage graves (Ormiegill, Camster Round, and Unstan); in southern Scotland they are rare. The discoidal type, on the other hand, is chiefly concentrated in the Tweed basin, and has not been found north of the Cromarty Firth. Though the number of both types is small, the differing distributions may reflect the same kind of regional specialization that is apparent in other types of Secondary Neolithic material in Scotland.

The size of these knives, and particularly of the discoidal type, suggests that they were made from mined rather than from beach-pebble flint; and since there is no marked concentration of either type in the Buchan district of Aberdeenshire, the only source of massive flint in Scotland, it is likely that many of them were imported from the south, either from Yorkshire or even from the flint mines of East Anglia, near which the greatest density of discoidal knives has been recorded.

It may be suggested in passing that the well-known 'Pict's knives' of Shetland may constitute a specialized regional variant, in local material, of the same basic form. Though no Pict's knife has so far been found in a chambered tomb or other satisfactorily dateable context, the apparent

[1] Piggott, *Neolithic Cultures* (1954), 359.
[2] *Proc. Prehist. Soc. East Anglia*, VI (1929), 52.

association of hoards of these objects with polished stone axes[1] and with a stone adze [2] suggest that a neolithic date is at least probable.

Of the jet 'sliders', shuttle-shaped objects perforated with an oval or lenticular aperture and perhaps used to fasten a belt or sash, only three examples have been found in Scotland. Two come from Skye and Kintyre respectively,[3] the latter as a secondary deposit in the Clyde-Carlingford tomb at Beacharra. The third is a stray find from a peat-bog at Balgone, near North Berwick.[4] Though the western examples may be of Scottish material, the type occurs more commonly in England, where it is associated with burials of the Peterborough and Dorchester cultures.[5]

In considering the flint arrowheads of *petit-tranchet*-derivative form, generally regarded as a specific type of the Secondary Neolithic cultures, it must be borne in mind that no comprehensive study has been made of their distribution. However, in so far as the collections of the National Museum represent their relative density in various parts of the country, it is clear that they present a very different picture from the leaf-shaped arrowheads discussed above (p. 20). Like the latter, they occur almost entirely in eastern areas, from the Beauly Firth to the Border, and only a bare score of specimens has been found in the west and north. But unlike the leaf form, there is no marked concentration in the north-east, apart from the single site of the Culbin Sands. Elsewhere they occur in large numbers only in the Tweed basin, where they actually outnumber the leaf form by about seven to two. In the counties of Banff, Aberdeen, Kincardine, and Angus, on the other hand, the leaf shape occurs over thirty times as often as the *petit-tranchet*-derivative. The restricted distribution of the type thus matches that of the discoidal flint knives; and in view of its scarcity near the principal source of flint in Aberdeenshire, it may perhaps best be regarded as exotic to Scotland, even though many of the specimens in the Tweed basin are undoubtedly of local flint.[6]

The Secondary Neolithic material discussed above can thus all plausibly be regarded as intrusive, representing the northwards migration from England of cultures already fully formed before their expansion. In support of this view it may be noticed that the distribution of these types

[1] *Proc. Soc. Ant. Scot.*, XXIX (1894–95), 48–54.
[2] *Proc. Soc. Ant. Scot.*, LXXX (1945–46), 140–1.
[3] *Proc. Soc. Ant. Scot.*, L (1915–16), 221.
[4] *Proc. Soc. Ant. Scot.*, VI (1867–8), 107–8.
[5] Piggott, *Neolithic Cultures* (1954), 311.
[6] *Proc. Soc. Ant. Scot.*, LXXXI (1946–47), 181–2.

(fig. 4) conforms very little to the recorded pattern of mesolithic settlement in Scotland, and that they do not occur at all on the coast of Argyll, in the Forth Valley or around the head-waters of the Clyde and Tweed. It is only indeed in the middle and lower areas of the Tweed basin that any substantial overlap can be seen.

It is possible, however, to distinguish elements in the Secondary Neolithic material of Scotland which appear to be indigenous, or at least mainly if not entirely of Scottish origin. These comprise the Sandhill type of pottery, and two forms of stone object: carved stone balls and cylindrically perforated maceheads. The latter are plotted in figs. 5 and 6.

Sandhill pottery has been recovered in quantity only from three coastal sites, the Luce Sands in Wigtownshire and the Gullane and Hedderwick Sands in East Lothian.[1] The wares are very variable in shape, fabric, and decoration, and no comprehensive study of the material has so far been made. Two shapes appear, however, to be noticeably frequent; a hemispherical bowl with plain rim, sometimes slightly inturned, decorated with coarse cord-impressions; and a larger and coarser barrel-shaped jar, with flat base and flattened rim, decorated with irregular linear patterns scored with a point or with a bird bone, the latter giving a shallow double groove. At Glenluce trial excavations by the writer in 1951 showed that these wares were contemporary with fragments of cord-zoned Beaker; and a similar association appears to have existed on the East Lothian sites.

Generically this pottery may be compared with the Sandhill wares of Northern Ireland,[2] and there are indeed resemblances of a specific kind as well. But even the material from Glenluce, when seen in bulk, has its own characteristics which distinguish it from comparable assemblages on the other side of the North Channel. The Sandhill wares of Scotland, therefore, though related to those of Ireland, may none the less be regarded as an indigenous phenomenon. It is on these sites, if anywhere, that we should seek for a survival of the traditions of the mesolithic strand-loopers of the Atlantic period.

The carved stone balls have often been discussed in the past,[3] generally

---

[1] *Proc. Soc. Ant. Scot.*, LXXXVI (1951–52), 43–69 (Glenluce); *ibid.*, XLII (1907–08), 308–19 (Gullane); *ibid.*, LIII (1928–29), 68–72 (Hedderwick). Much of the material from Glenluce has not been published.

[2] Piggott, *Neolithic Cultures* (1954), 317–21.

[3] *Proc. Soc. Ant. Scot.*, XI (1875–76), 29–62, 313–19; *ibid.*, XXXVI (1901–02), 11–16; *ibid.*, XLI (1916–07), 290–300; *ibid.*, XLVIII (1913–14), 407–20; *Proc. Roy. Soc. Edinburgh*, L (1929–30), 72–73.

without any firm conclusion, since apart from the specimens from Skara Brae[1] none has so far been found in satisfactory association with any other significant type of object. The assumption that these balls belong to the Secondary Neolithic culture of Scotland thus rests upon an admittedly slender foundation. But a date within the first half of the second millennium B.C. is supported by the spiral ornament on the examples from Towie, Aberdeenshire, from Elgin and from Glasterlaw, Forfarshire, which has been compared to motifs in the repertory of passage-grave 'art' of this period. Moreover, the distribution of carved stone balls accords well with that of the maceheads, whose Secondary Neolithic context is not in doubt.

The map in fig. 5 is based on the literature cited above and on a census of the unpublished examples in the principal Scottish museums. It includes about twice the number of sites previously plotted by Childe,[2] but excludes at least twenty specimens whose precise provenance is not recorded. Almost all of these come from somewhere in Aberdeenshire, so that the concentration of the type in that county is even more marked than the map itself suggests.

It will be noticed that south of the Clyde-Forth line carved stone balls are conspicuously absent from the areas in which 'intrusive' Secondary Neolithic material occurs (fig. 4), and especially from the basin of the Tweed, a deficiency which serves to underline all the more strongly the regional character of the concentration in Aberdeenshire.

The polished stone maceheads with cylindrical perforation, mapped in fig. 6, belong to types which have well-established Secondary Neolithic associations.[3] The remarkable density of these objects in Orkney (where curiously the greater number are broken specimens) comprises over 30 per cent of the total known in Scotland, and it is difficult not to assume a northern origin for the type. Though petrological examination has not been carried out systematically, it should be noted that two specimens of the 'cushion' type studied by Gibson,[4] found in Lewis and Fife, appear to be of a rock native to Shetland.[5]

Maceheads of these types are also widespread, of course, in England and Wales, and it would be foolish to suggest that they all originate north of the Border. But it should be remembered that almost all of them

[1] V. G. Childe, *Skara Brae* (1931), 100–9.
[2] *Proc. Roy. Soc. Edinburgh*, L (1929–30), 73.
[3] Piggott, *Neolithic Cultures* (1954), 285, 353, 354.
[4] *Proc. Soc. Ant. Scot.*, LXXVIII (1943–44), 16–25.
[5] *Proc. Soc. Ant. Scot.*, LXVIII (1933–34), 428–32.

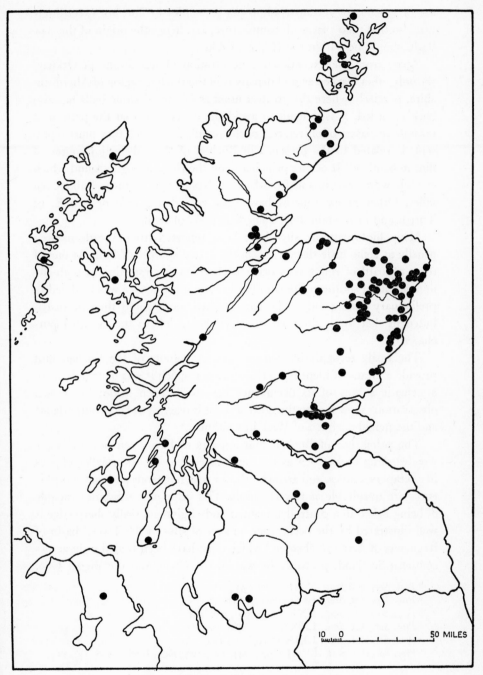

Fig. 5. Distribution of carved stone balls.

are of igneous or metamorphic rocks (examples in flint are exceedingly rare), so that their places of manufacture, and hence the origin of the type itself, should lie within the Highland Zone.

Apart from the exceptional concentration of maceheads in Orkney, the only other marked area of density is in the Buchan region of Aberdeenshire, precisely where the greatest number of carved stone balls has also been recorded. It is difficult to avoid the conclusion that the pattern of both these classes of object, and of the population which they must represent, is related to the presence in Buchan of the only major source of flint in Scotland. It occurs principally on the ridge of high ground which extends westwards inland from Buchan Ness for a distance of about ten miles. Other minor sources have been recorded a mile or two E. of Turriff and in Boyndie Bay, immediately W. of Banff.[1]

Many flint-knapping sites have been reported from Aberdeenshire,[2] usually at some little distance from the actual sources of flint. At one of these a hoard of rough-outs occurred,[3] which suggests that as with the mined flint of southern England fabrication at the source was confined to preliminary flaking only. The part-finished tools would then be distributed in that form, the final processes being left to the eventual purchaser.

The easily recognizable red and orange colours of the Buchan flint provide a means of identifying the area over which it was distributed. No systematic survey of its occurrence has so far been made; but casual observations show that to the north at least it reached as far as Sutherland[4] and the neighbourhood of Wick in Caithness.[5]

The prime use of Buchan flint appears to have been not for heavy woodworking tools, such as axes and adzes, but for the smaller objects like scrapers, knives, and arrowheads, for which igneous and metamorphic rocks are unsuitable as raw materials. The value of a substance capable of being flaked in a controlled manner and of giving a really sharp edge is well illustrated by the occurrence on several sites in the Tweed basin of fragments of Arran pitchstone,[6] which must have been traded right across southern Scotland, probably by way of the Clyde and the Biggar Gap.

[1] *Proc. Soc. Ant. Scot.*, X (1872–73), 514–18.
[2] *Proc. Soc. Ant. Scot.*, LI (1916–17), 117–27.
[3] *Proc. Soc. Ant. Scot.*, XXX (1895–96), 346–51.
[4] *Proc. Soc. Ant. Scot.*, LXXX (1945–46), 32.
[5] *Proc. Soc. Ant. Scot.*, LXIX (1934–35), 114.
[6] *Proc. Soc. Ant. Scot.*, LVIII (1923–24), 120, 123; *ibid.*, LXI (1926–27), 114.

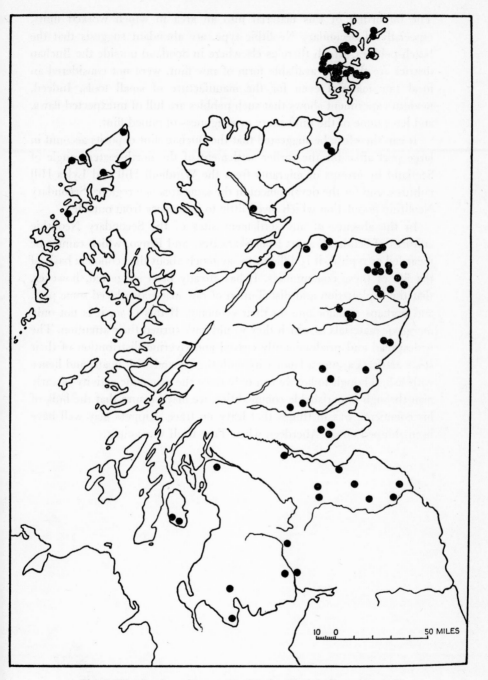

Fig. 6. Distribution of stone maceheads cylindrically perforated.

The importing of this material into an area in which worked flints, especially of Secondary Neolithic type, are abundant suggests that the beach-pebbles, which there as elsewhere in Scotland outside the Buchan district are the only available form of raw flint, were not considered an ideal raw material even for the manufacture of small tools. Indeed, modern experiment shows that such pebbles are full of unexpected flaws, and have none of the uniformity or toughness of mined flint.

It can therefore be suggested that the Buchan flint deposits account in large part alike for the earlier settlement of the north-eastern angle of Scotland by groups of migrants from the Windmill Hill and Lyles Hill cultures, and for the development in the same area of a regional Secondary Neolithic population which owed little to influences from outside.

In the absence of any settlement sites of the Secondary Neolithic cultures of Scotland, apart from Skara Brae and Rinyo, which cannot be regarded as typical, it is difficult to say much about the economic basis of the life of these communities. It has already been suggested, however, that the exploitation and distribution of raw materials played some part, and perhaps a major one, in their economy. If this is so, it is not only *inorganic* materials to which they would have turned their attention. The widespread and predominantly coastal and riverine distribution of their stone artifacts argues a familiarity with the sea and with boats, and hence with fish. Though today we can only trace the economic activity of early man through imperishable commodities, we may be sure that the bulk of his commerce was in things that leave no trace. Kippers may well have been shipped out of Aberdeen when Troy itself was young.

Appendix

The Scottish finds of pottery and other objects plotted in figs. 1, 2, and 4 are listed hereunder.

FIG. 1

Lugged bowls of Piggott's forms A, B, and C

Loanhead of Daviot, Aberdeenshire — *Proc. Soc. Ant. Scot.*, LXIX (1934–35), 168–214, fig. 14, no. 12.

East Finnercy, Aberdeenshire — *Proc. Soc. Ant. Scot.*, LXIII (1928–29), 62–63, fig. 50, nos. 6 and 7.

Cairnpapple, West Lothian — *Proc. Soc. Ant. Scot.*, LXXXII (1947–48), 102, fig. 15, no. 2.

Beacharra, Kintyre, Argyll — *Proc. Soc. Ant. Scot.*, LXIII (1928–29), 51–53, fig. 28.

Torlin, Arran — *Proc. Soc. Ant. Scot.*, LXIII (1928–29), 46, fig. 15.

Clachaig, Arran — *Proc. Soc. Ant. Scot.*, LXIII (1928–29), 46, fig. 16.

Sliddery Water, Arran — *Proc. Soc. Ant. Scot.*, LXIII (1928–29), 47, fig. 18.

Luce Sands, Wigtownshire — *Proc. Soc. Ant. Scot.*, LXIII (1928–29), 66, no. 28, fig. 44, no. 23; *ibid.*, LXVII (1932–33), 240, no. 15, fig. 6, no. 11.

Shouldered bowls of Piggott's Form G

Powsode Cairn, Atherb, Aberdeenshire — Unpublished. Nat. Mus., Edinburgh, nos. EO 910, 923.

Bantaskine, Stirlingshire — *Proc. Soc. Ant. Scot.*, LXIII (1928–29), 56–57, fig. 38, no. 8.

Cairnpapple, West Lothian   *Proc. Soc. Ant. Scot.*, **LXXXII** (1947–48), 102, fig. 15, no. 1.

Cairnholy I, Kirkcudbright   *Proc. Soc. Ant. Scot.*, **LXXXIII** (1948–49), 118–19, fig. 7, no. 1.

FIG. 2

Lyles Hill Ware

Urquhart, Morayshire   *Proc. Soc. Ant. Scot.*, **LXXX** (1945–46), 142, Pl. XXIV, no. 1.

Townhead, Rothesay, Bute   *Proc. Soc. Ant. Scot.*, **LXIII** (1928–29), 57–59, fig. 39.

Cairnholy I, Kirkcudbright   *Proc. Soc. Ant. Scot.*, **LXXXIII** (1948–49), 119, fig. 7, no. 2.

Lyles Hill Ware with finger-tip fluting

Easterton of Roseisle, Morayshire   *Proc. Soc. Ant. Scot.*, **LXIII** (1928–29), 56, figs. 37, 38.

Spey Valley, between Grantown and Newtonmore   *Proc. Soc. Ant. Scot.*, **LXXI** (1936–37), 367.

Powsode Cairn, Atherb, Aberdeenshire   Unpublished. Nat. Mus., Edinburgh, no. EO 917.

Knapperty Hillock, Auchmachar, Aberdeenshire   *Proc. Soc. Ant. Scot.*, **LXIII** (1928–29), 63.

Loanhead of Daviot, Aberdeenshire   *Proc. Soc. Ant. Scot.*, **LXIX** (1934–35), 207, fig. 14, type 6, nos. 2–4.

East Finnercy, Aberdeenshire   Unpublished. Report forthcoming in *Proc. Soc. Ant. Scot.*

Cultoquhey, Crieff, Perthshire   Unpublished. Information from Professor Stuart Piggott.

Achnachree, Benderloch, Argyll   *Proc. Soc. Ant. Scot.*, **LXIII** (1928–29), 38, fig. 3.

Kilchoan, Poltalloch, Argyll   *Proc. Soc. Ant. Scot.*, **LXIII** (1928–29), 38.

Nether Largie, Poltalloch, Argyll   *Proc. Soc. Ant. Scot.*, **LXIII** (1928–29), 37, fig. 1.

Glecknabae, Bute	*Proc. Soc. Ant. Scot.*, LXIII (1928–29), 49–50, figs. 22, 23.
Knappers, Clydebank, Dumbartonshire	*Proc. Soc. Ant. Scot.*, LXXXII (1947–48), 236, fig. 1, no. 2.
Whitemoss, Bishopton, Renfrewshire	Unpublished. Information from Professor Stuart Piggott.
Luce Sands, Wigtownshire	*Proc. Soc. Ant. Scot.*, LXIII (1928–29), 66, nos. 13, 18, 20.

FIG. 4

Peterborough Ware

Scotstarvit, Fife	*Proc. Soc. Ant. Scot.*, LXXXII (1947–48), 262.
Knappers, Clydebank, Dumbartonshire	*Proc. Soc. Ant. Scot.*, LXIX (1934–35), 363–4.
Hedderwick Sands, East Lothian	*Proc. Soc. Ant. Scot.*, LXIII (1928–29), 92, fig. 55, nos. 4–7.
Scremerston Hill, near Berwick-on-Tweed, Northumberland	Unpublished. Nat. Mus., Edinburgh.
Ford Castle, Northumberland	*Arch. Journ.*, LXXXVIII (1931), 157.
Shewalton Sands, Irvine, Ayrshire	*Proc. Prehist. Soc.*, XVII (1951), 53.
Cairnholy I, Kirkcudbright	*Proc. Soc. Ant. Scot.*, LXXXIII (1948–49), 120, no. 7.
Luce Sands, Wigtownshire	*Proc. Soc. Ant. Scot.*, LXIII (1928–29), 92, fig. 55, nos. 1–3, 8.

Rinyo Clacton Ware

Rinyo, Rousay, Orkney	*Proc. Soc. Ant. Scot.*, LXXIII (1938–39), 22–25; *ibid.*, LXXXI (1946–47), 34–39.
Evie, Orkney	*Proc. Soc. Ant. Scot.*, LXXX (1945–46), 143.
Dingieshow, Deerness, Orkney	*Proc. Soc. Ant. Scot.*, LXXX (1945–46), 142.

Skara Brae, Orkney	Childe, *Skara Brae* (1931), 127–34.
Freswick Sands, Caithness	*Proc. Prehist. Soc.*, XVII (1951), 73.
Unival, North Uist	*Proc. Soc. Ant. Scot.*, LXXXII (1947–48), 26–28.
Tentsmuir, Fife	Unpublished. St. Andrews University Museum.
Gullane Sands, East Lothian	*Proc. Soc. Ant. Scot.*, XLII (1907–8), 312–15.
Hedderwick Sands, East Lothian	*Proc. Soc. Ant. Scot.*, LXXX (1945–46), 143, fig. 1, no. 5.
Knappers, Clydebank, Dumbartonshire	*Proc. Soc. Ant. Scot.*, LXXXIV (1949–50), 180–3.
Townhead, Rothesay, Bute	*Proc. Soc. Ant. Scot.*, LXXXIV (1949–50), 183.
Tormore, Arran	Piggott, *Neolithic Cultures* (1954), 386.
Luce Sands, Wigtownshire	*Proc. Soc. Ant. Scot.*, LXXX (1945–46), 143.
Old Yeavering, Wooler, Northumberland	Unpublished. Information from Dr. Brian Hope-Taylor.

Polished Flint Knives

Rinyo, Rousay, Orkney	*Proc. Soc. Ant. Scot.*, LXXIII (1938–39), 27, fig. 8, no. 11.
Unstan, Orkney	*Proc. Soc. Ant. Scot.*, XIX (1884–85), 350.
Skara Brae, Orkney	Childe, *Skara Brae* (1931), 114, fig. 10.
Camster Round Cairn, Caithness	Anderson, *Scotland in Pagan Times: Bronze and Stone Ages* (1886), 252, fig. 251.
Ormiegill, Ulbster, Caithness	Anderson, *op. cit.*, 247, fig. 244.
Urquhart, Morayshire	*Proc. Soc. Ant. Scot.*, IX (1870–71), 238, fig. 1.
Urquhart, Morayshire	Unpublished. Nat. Mus., Edinburgh.

Fintray, Aberdeenshire	Unpublished. Nat. Mus., Edinburgh.
Blelack, Cromar, Aberdeenshire	*Proc. Soc. Ant. Soc.*, IX (1870–71), 239.
Birse, Aberdeenshire	Unpublished. Nat. Mus., Edinburgh.
Overhowden, Channelkirk, Berwickshire	*Proc. Soc. Ant. Scot.*, LXVI (1931–32), 25, fig. 8.
Strachur, Argyll	*Proc. Soc. Ant. Scot.*, IX (1870–71), 239, fig. 2.
Tormore, Arran	*Proc. Soc. Ant. Scot.*, XXXVI (1901–2), 101, fig. 25.
Whiting Bay, Arran	Unpublished. Nat. Mus., Edinburgh.

Discoidal Flint Knives

Ardross, Easter Ross	Unpublished. Nat. Mus., Edinburgh.
Culbin Sands, Morayshire	*Proc. Soc. Ant. Scot.*, XXV (1890–91), 498–9.
Marnoch, Banffshire	Unpublished. Nat. Mus., Edinburgh.
Pitdoulzie, Turriff, Aberdeenshire	*Proc. Soc. Ant. Scot.*, XII (1876–77), 207.
Leslie, Aberdeenshire	Unpublished. Nat. Mus., Edinburgh.
Kintore, Aberdeenshire	Evans, *Anc. Stone Implements*, 2nd ed. (1897), 342.
Fourdoun, Kincardineshire	*Proc. Soc. Ant. Scot.*, XI (1874–75), 576.
Fordoun, Kincardineshire	Unpublished. Nat. Mus., Edinburgh.
Airhouse, Channelkirk, Berwickshire	*Proc. Soc. Ant. Scot.*, LXII (1927–28) 170.
Ninewar, Duns, Berwickshire [1]	*Proc. Soc. Ant. Scot.*, LXII (1927–28), 172.

[1] Polished discoidal scraper.

Birkenside, Lauder, Berwickshire	Unpublished. Nat. Mus., Edinburgh.
Earlston, Berwickshire	*Proc. Soc. Ant. Scot.*, XXVIII (1893–94), 324.
Butterlaw, Coldstream, Berwickshire	*Proc. Soc. Ant. Scot.*, XXVIII (1893–94), 324.
Whooplaw, Stow, Roxburghshire	*Proc. Soc. Ant. Scot.*, LI (1916–17), 234.
Blackhaugh, Clovenfords, Selkirkshire	*Proc. Soc. Ant. Scot.*, LXXIV (1939–40), 10.
Milton Loch, Kirkcudbright	Unpublished. Nat. Mus., Edinburgh.
Luce Sands, Wigtownshire	*Proc. Soc. Ant. Scot.*, XXIII (1888–89), 204.

1. Obanian tools of antler, bone and stone. (Chap. I).

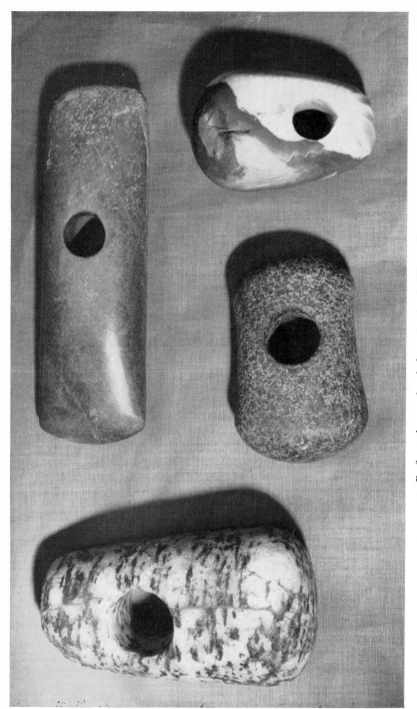

2. Perforated mace-heads from Scotland. (Chap. I).

3. Carved stone balls from Scotland. (Chap. I).

4(a). Stenness stone circle, Orkney. (Chap. II).

4(b). Interior of Maes Howe, Orkney. (Chap. II).

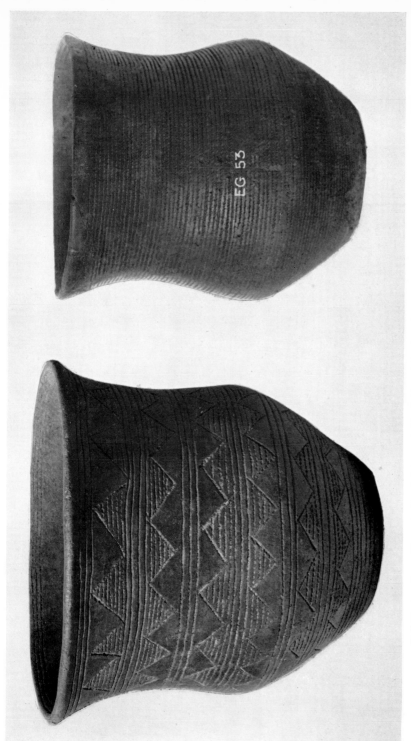

5. Bell-Beaker from Fingask, Perthshire and Cord-Zoned Beaker from Bathgate, West Lothian. (Chap. III).

6. Beakers from Edzel (left) and Ermelo, Netherlands (right). (Chap. III).

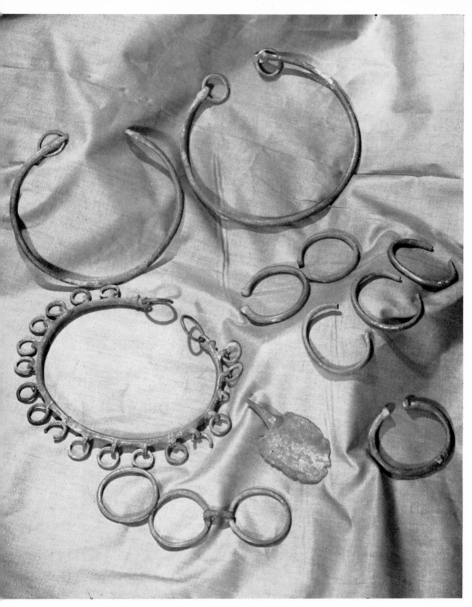

7. Late Bronze Age hoard. Braes of Gight. (Chap. IV).

8. Late Bronze Age bucket, Cardross. (Chap. IV).

CHAPTER TWO

The Megalith Builders

So much has been written about the megalithic monuments of Scotland, particularly in the last twenty-five years, that any fresh account of them at the moment can do little to supplement the comprehensive treatment of the subject provided by Childe in his *Prehistory of Scotland* (1935) and Piggott in his *Neolithic Cultures of the British Isles* (1954), and the reader is directed to these two books and the detailed references they contain at every turn of the description and discussion attempted in this present chapter. Yet because so much has been written about this important and interesting subject—and on any showing the megalith builders must be one of the main ethnic elements in the early peopling of Scotland—and because the books of Childe and Piggott we have mentioned, themselves separated by nearly twenty years, are in themselves stages in the history of archaeological scholarship in Scotland, it may be convenient and profitable here first to survey some of the major attempts made at synthesizing our knowledge of the Scottish megalithic monuments. We can then see present orthodoxies and heresies in the perspective of our growing knowledge of Scottish prehistory and of the megalithic monuments of Europe in general. It should be said here that in this chapter our main concern is with megalithic tombs, but brief reference is made at the end to other types of megalithic monument in Scotland.

There is no need, for our present historical purpose, to go farther back than Daniel Wilson, one of the pioneers of Scottish, and for that matter European prehistory: indeed, it was Wilson who introduced the word prehistory into the English language—and not, surprisingly, his predecessors like the Wessex fieldworkers Colt Hoare and Cunnington or the Danish historians and archaeologists Vedel-Simonsen and Christian Thomsen, who propounded the ideas of successive ages of stone, bronze, and iron in the most ancient history of man. Daniel Wilson published in 1851 his *Archaeology and Prehistoric Annals of Scotland*, and there refers to 'the application of the term prehistoric—introduced if I mistake not, for the first time in this work'. This term was not readily received with enthusiasm by all workers in the field of early Scottish archaeology: how scornful, for example, was James Fergusson of the term prehistory. He quoted the title of Wilson's book in his *Rude Stone Monuments* and added 'whatever that may mean',[1] and Robert Munro, as late as 1899 was referring to 'that obscure period in the history of Scotland vaguely defined as the *prehistoric*'.[2]

Daniel Wilson very naturally had to discuss the chambered cairns and cromlechs of Scotland, and he set these against his picture of Scottish prehistory which he divided into the primeval or stone period, the archaic or bronze period, the iron period and the Christian period. He figured some cromlechs as he called them, using the common Welsh folk name for a megalithic tomb, and also Wideford Hill in Orkney, which was, however, to him, not a tomb but a Pict's house. Wilson had no doubt as to the sepulchral nature of the chambered tombs and cromlechs, thinking this had been proved by F. C. Lukis and John Bell. They were all part of his monolithic era of the primeval or stone period. He did not think them Celtic monuments as others did, but 'the work of an elder race of whose language we have little reason to believe any relic has survived to the present day'. The chambered cairns he thought were 'catacombs of the whole tribe . . . the memorial of the victors on some bloody battle field'. One thing Daniel Wilson did not find surprising at all, and that is the absence of contemporary settlement sites; it was normal he thought that the dead should be well provided for and that the houses of the living should perish; death and religion, he insisted, were probably more important to primitive peoples than life. The ordinary houses of the megalith builders would, of course, have perished, in Wilson's view.

[1] James Fergusson, *Rude Stone Monuments in All Countries: Their Ages and Uses*, London, 1872, 239.
[2] Robert Munro, *Prehistoric Scotland and its Place in European Civilisation*, Edinburgh and London, 1899, v.

The same sort of view was held by the two Scottish scholars who, between Wilson himself and modern scholars, did most to advance Scottish archaeology and synthesize Scottish prehistory—namely Robert Munro and Joseph Anderson, two remarkable men who both lived to be well over eighty and who spanned in their archaeological lives the whole development of nineteenth-century Scottish archaeology and the whole gamut of its changing perspectives. Joseph Anderson came of age two years after Daniel Wilson's *Prehistoric Annals* was first published—it was incidentally the year that also saw the publication of Beddoe's *Scottish Ethnology*: while Robert Munro died in 1920, five years before the publication of Childe's *Dawn of European Civilisation* and Kendrick's *Axe Age*. This long span of three-quarters of a century had seen the first excavations in Scottish megalithic monuments. George Petrie had excavated Wideford Hill in 1849, and it was his plan that Wilson had published. In 1851 a Captain Thomas excavated a monument on the Holm of Papa Westray in Orkney, which he described as 104 feet long by 41 feet broad by 10 feet high. It consists of a passage leading in from the middle of the south side of a long mound, and a long chamber at right-angles to this with no less than fourteen side-chambers opening out of it. Thomas found no artifacts and no bones except a few of sheep and rabbit. He recorded some engravings on the stones and others were found a few years later by Petrie. Nearly a hundred years later the Royal Commission on the Ancient Monuments of Scotland, in their *Inventory of Orkney*, suggest very plausibly that in two places these engravings are 'crude representations of the human face similar to that found on the chalk drums from Folkton, Yorkshire'.[1] This face motif on the Holm of Papa Westray is not only to be compared with that on the chalk idols from Folkton, but with the face on the roof stone of the north side-chamber at New Grange, the faces on the underside of the capstone of the Déhus in Guernsey, the chalk-cut tombs of Coizard and Courjeonnet in the Marne, the statue-menhirs of southern France, and the pottery and portable idols of the south Iberian collective tombs. It provides a link, tenuous, slight, but none the less sure, between the megalith builders of the extreme north of the British Isles and their ultimate progenitors, as we shall see most people now believe, in the Mediterranean. But this connexion, which makes an exciting historical context out of the archaeological detail of these dead tombs, was not apparent to the Scottish antiquaries of the mid-nineteenth

[1] *Inventory of Orkney*, Edinburgh, 1946, 189.

century, who were still in the process of discovering the megalithic tombs of their native land.

In 1861 an even more exciting tomb than the Holm of Papa Westray was discovered; this was Maes Howe in the Orkneys, which Daniel Wilson had characterized as 'the Wiltshire of Scotland, in so far as the mere number of sepulchral mounds along with megalithic groups and other aboriginal structures can constitute this distinction'. This fine monument, which the Royal Commission on the Ancient Monuments of Scotland describe with pardonable pride as 'the supreme example of its class in Great Britain',[1] is a corbelled passage grave with three side-chambers set in a round mound 24 feet high by 115 feet in diameter. The mound itself is surrounded by a berm and this by a broad ditch averaging 45 feet in width and 6 feet in depth. James Farrer, M.P., when he excavated the mound in 1861, found no artifacts or bones, but he did find that the tomb had been broken into previously and that records of this survived on various stones of the chamber in the form of twenty-four runic inscriptions as well as three engraved figures of a walrus, a dragon, and a serpent knot. Professor Haakon Shetelig dates these engravings to the early twelfth century A.D. The runic inscriptions were apparently made on different occasions: two inscriptions refer to the breaking in of the Howe by Crusaders, and these are usually identified with the expedition of Earl Rognvald and Eindrid the Younger, which wintered in Orkney in 1150–51. Another visit took place in January 1153, where Earl Harold and his men landed near Stromness and were in the *orkahaugr*, presumably Maes Howe, 'while a snowstorm drove over them and there two men of their band lost their wits, and that was a great hindrance to the journey'. Several of the runic inscriptions refer to treasure being found there: one says 'treasure was carried off in the course of three nights', another 'a long time ago was a great treasure hidden here . . . Haakon single-handed bore treasure from this howe', and a third 'treasure was carried off before those Crusaders broke into the howe'.[2] These references, while not specific, seem very circumstantial and can hardly be dismissed as part of a general folk feeling in Viking times that there was treasure to be found in

[1] *Inventory of Orkney*, 306. Farrer's *Maeshowe* was privately printed in 1802. For an account of recent excavations at the site see V. G. Childe, *Proc. Soc. Ant. Scot.*, LXXXVIII (1956), 155–72.

[2] These translations of the runes are from Bruce Dickins, *Proc. Orkney Ant. Soc.*, VIII (1929–30), 27–30. See also J. Farrer, *Notice of Runic Inscriptions . . . in the Orkneys*, Edinburgh, 1862, and *Inventory of Orkney*, 308–13.

all ancient burial mounds. It does seem that the twelfth-century Vikings who broke into Maes Howe did find something of value. However that may be, they certainly left nothing of value for Farrer to find seven centuries later.[1]

We have already quoted one dictum of the Royal Commission on Ancient Monuments in Scotland on Maes Howe; elsewhere they refer to it as a 'magnificent domed tomb . . . probably without a rival in Western Europe',[2] and they do well, as Childe has done on several occasions, to draw attention to some of the very remarkable features that exist at Maes Howe—not only the berm and the encircling ditch which we have already mentioned, but the almost ashlar-like dressing of the walling stones, the brilliant masonry of the jointing, the three side-chambers set not on the ground but high up in the walls, and most of all the anglepiers of what is in plan a square chamber. Without any doubt, Maes Howe is a *tour de force* of prehistoric architecture in western Europe.[3]

Three years after Farrer's discovery and excavation of Maes Howe, Canon Greenwell was digging in the Kilmartin and Kilmichael area of Argyllshire in tombs we would now describe as south-west Scottish segmented long cists or gallery graves. In 1865 and 1866 Anderson was excavating a series of chambered cairns in Caithness; in 1867 Farrer and Petrie dug the Quoyness monument in Sanday in the Orkneys; in 1871 Dr. Angus Smith excavated the chambered cairn of Achnacree near Loch Etive in Argyll, and in 1884 Clouston dug Unstan. The men who, like Munro and Anderson, attempted to synthesize Scottish prehistory at the end of the nineteenth century were in quite a different position from Daniel Wilson in 1851. They now had a considerable number of excavations to turn to; they had accounts of different types of tombs in different parts of Scotland, and what is equally important, since our knowledge of megaliths or indeed of any class of monument can only advance by comparative study outside a country as well as excavation and analysis within it, they were beginning to learn something of similar monuments outside Scotland. The Baron Bonstetten's *Essai sur les dolmens* had appeared in 1865, James Fergusson's *Rude Stone Monuments* was published seven

---

[1] On the question of the Maes Howe 'treasure' see Piggott, *Neolithic Cultures of the British Isles* (Cambridge, 1954), 253–4. [2] *Report and Introduction to Inventory of Orkney and Shetland* (Edinburgh, 1946), 19. [3] The large stones for blocking the entrances to the side-chambers are another extraordinary feature. In some ways Maes Howe reminds one of Iberian tombs like Tutugi and not the collective chambered tombs of the early second millennium. Alcalar in south Portugal has, of course, parallels for the cupboard-like side-chambers.

years later; its frontispiece was the Standing Stones of Stennis, and he devoted a whole chapter to the Scottish megaliths, expressing his indebtedness for information about them to John Stuart of Edinburgh and to Sir Henry Dryden, the latter a man well travelled in western Europe in search of megaliths.

James Fergusson was astonishingly complacent about the state of knowledge at the time when he wrote: 'Whatever may be the case as regards Ireland, it is probable that the megalithic remains of Scotland are all known and have been described more or less in detail'. His own account of Scotland is very thin, but his explanation of the origins of the Scottish megaliths very full and definite; they were the work of two groups of people, a 'circle building race' who came from Scandinavia between 800 and 1,000 A.D. [sic] and spread southwards from the Orkneys, where they had built Stennis and Maes Howe, and a 'dolmen-building race' who had spread up from Ireland and Wales and were derived from the builders of the megalithic monuments of Brittany which Fergusson dated to 'the Arthurian age—between 380 and 550 A.D.' We need not spend much time on Fergusson's ideas except to realize that for long his was the only general book dealing with megalithic monuments as a whole, and that as a result his views had a wide currency, and that the fact he was able to put forward views on dating which to us at the present day seem totally without any foundation whatsoever was some indication of the real ignorance of comparative megalithic scholarship in and out of Scotland three-quarters of a century ago.

Let us now see what sort of a synthesis was made by Anderson and Munro, who knew far more about the Scottish material than Fergusson did and who were unconvinced by his chronological arguments. Between 1879 and 1882 Anderson was asked to give the Rhind Lectures by the Society of Antiquaries of Scotland. These lectures had been founded from the estate of Henry Rhind of Sibster, who had himself excavated four chambered barrows at Yarhouse in Caithness. Anderson's lectures were published four years later as *Scotland in Pagan Times; the Bronze and Stone Ages*. Looking back at the two chapters of this book which deal with Scottish chambered cairns, the present writer finds it most remarkable to see what a grasp Anderson had of the problem.[1] He first describes monu-

---

[1] But then Joseph Anderson was a most remarkable man. It is worth reading the articles he wrote on archaeological subjects for the 1888–92 edition of *Chambers's Encyclopaedia*.

ments in Caithness and notes that there are two types—long, horned cairns and round cairns; he describes monuments in Argyll and says of them 'we recognize the same essential features of construction and contents that give typical character to the Caithness cairns'; he discusses some of the Orkney monuments and found Maes Howe as having 'some title to be classed as a local variety'.

Anderson's general picture was that all the Scottish chambered barrows should be considered as variants of one structural type 'however much they may differ from each other in the minor details of external form or internal arrangement'; and that this basic type belonged to the Stone Age. He inferred that the long barrow did not continue into the Bronze Age, but that the round-chambered barrow did. He was quite obviously enormously impressed by the long barrows of Wiltshire and the Cotswolds, comparing the Caithness horned cairns with Ablington, Belas Knap, Avening, and Eyford. All, he declared, 'exhibit more or less of the same general character', and, 'in view of the excessively pronounced peculiarities of that character, there is no escape from the inference that they are all the work of one race of men'. And he quoted with great approval the words of Professor Rolleston that 'the peculiarities of a horn cairn are such that it is impossible to imagine that they do not indicate to us that one race of men, and only one, must have combined them as they are combined. And their geographical distribution shows with equal conclusiveness that of whatever stock that race may have been, they were a homogeneous people spread over the whole area of Britain'. We shall see later how much the present writer is in sympathy with this Anderson-Rolleston point of view which has had little support in the last quarter century.

Robert Munro's *Prehistoric Scotland* was published in 1899 as a general introduction to a series of county histories of Scotland, and we find here the same material being gone over as Anderson dealt with in his Rhind lectures—Caithness, Orkney, Achnacree, and the Clava tombs, but without any fresh conclusions emerging, except that the cairns were Bronze Age in date. Munro seemed specially exercised by the presence of cremation in Scottish chambered tombs; in another place he says that 'in the counties of Argyll, Inverness, Sutherland, Caithness and the Orkneys it has been conclusively proved that cremation and inhumation were carried on simultaneously', and that this showed 'that the custom of constructing chambered cairns travelled slowly northwards and was overtaken by that of cremation'. These words were first written by Munro in 1913; I quote them from the fifth edition of his book *Prehistoric Britain*, published in the Home University Library in 1928, which I read as a schoolboy interested in archaeology. This fifth edition appeared three years after a book which virtually revolutionized European prehistory—Gordon Childe's *Dawn of European Civilisation*. In this remarkable book Childe set the picture of European prehistory in terms which no one working in the British Isles had had readily available to them before. He summarized what was really known about megalithic monuments in western Europe; no one writing after this book about Scottish chambered tombs could write in the contexts of Anderson and Munro.[1] This is not to say that no substantial advances were made in the study of Scottish megalithic tombs between Anderson's Rhind Lectures of 1882 and 1927, when Childe was appointed the first holder of the Abercromby Chair of Prehistoric Archaeology in Edinburgh. One person in particular had done a very great deal in the way of accurate field survey and description; this was Professor T. H. Bryce, who in a series of articles in the *Proceedings of the Society of Antiquaries of Scotland* and in a fine chapter on Sepulchral Remains in *The Book of Arran*, provided us with the first full account of the twenty-odd sites in Arran and Bute of which some, like Carn Ban, East Bennan, Whiting Bay, and Slidderie in Arran, have become as classic in the literature as were the Orkney and Caithness sites we have already mentioned.[2] Bryce saw the spread of chambered tombs as a unitary affair from the Mediterranean; indeed, he thought that what he called 'the Iberian origin of the Long Barrow people and chamber builders' was a fact which went back to Tacitus's description of the western tribes of Britain. Writing in the style and with the perspective with which Rice Holmes was writing in southern Britain at the time, he saw the chambered tomb builders spreading from Iberia along the west coasts of France, and then, by two routes 'first along the English channel and thence to the

---

[1] The gap between the Anderson-Munro régime and the Childe régime in Scottish archaeology is the gap which yawned in European archaeology as a whole. In England it is the gap between Pitt Rivers and Wheeler, Fox, Childe, and Crawford. In France it is the gap between G. de Mortillet and Déchelette and the present day.

[2] Bryce's papers on Arran are in *Proc. Soc. Ant. Scot.*, XXXVI (1901–02), 74–181; XXXVII (1902–03), 36–37; and XLIII (1908–09), 337–70; and on Bute in the same, XXXVIII (1903–04), 17–81. *The Book of Arran* (Glasgow, 1910) was edited by J. A. Balfour; Bryce's chapter is pp. 33–155.

Baltic, and second over to Ireland and up St George's Channel. The first stream hardly touched England but spread on to the Baltic; the second spent itself chiefly on Ireland . . . the chamber builders came from the south-west and spread over the Hebrides to the Pentland Firth and the Orkneys, and possibly also up the Great Glen to the Moray Firth.'[1]

This was being written in 1910. Twenty-one years later the new Professor of Prehistoric Archaeology read a paper to the Glasgow Archaeological Society; it was the first time Professor Childe had set out his views about Scottish megalithic tombs in public. It was published two years later and in the view of the present writer was one of the most important contributions ever made to the theory of megaliths as well as to our understanding of Scottish megalithic architecture.[2] In this paper Childe set out two principles and the first was a guide to the typology of megalithic tombs in which he said: 'The oldest types will be most accurately reproduced in the greatest number of distinct regions; types localized in specific areas will be later inasmuch as they represent regional variants on the original type or types. Moreover, in any given area, it might be expected that the older types would be concentrated around one or more foci while later variants might have a wider distribution'. The second general observation was that there were in north-western Europe two principal sorts of plan, 'not necessarily unrelated in the long run': these were the passage grave and what Childe called 'a long cist or covered gallery'—this second class is now usually referred to as a gallery grave.

The second general observation of Childe's was a revolutionary one as far as the study of megalithic tombs in western Europe was concerned. Hitherto these tombs had been classified, if at all, according to the Montelian threefold system usually rendered into English as dolmen, passage grave, and gallery grave (or long cist), and this had been thought of, not merely as a taxonomic device, but also as a typological device; the dolmen-passage grave-gallery grave series was conceived of as a sequence. This threefold sequence was certainly used to interpret the Iberian megalithic tombs; it was also applied to the French megalithic material and is still so applied.[3] It was perhaps the good fortune of the Scottish material that

[1] Bryce in (ed. Balfour) *The Book of Arran*, 98–99.

[2] V. G. Childe, 'Scottish Megalithic Tombs and their Affinities', *Trans. Glas. Arch. Soc.*, new ser. VIII (1933), 121–37.

[3] As for example by Arnal, *Bull.Soc.Préhist.Franc.*, 1956, 518; and Giot, *Menhirs et Dolmens*, Chateaulin, 1957.

much of it is aberrant and local and does not readily fall into the passage-grave and gallery-grave classic categories, and that there are hardly any 'dolmens' in the Montelian sense in Scotland, so that the threefold sequence was hardly ever applied to Scotland.[1] Childe suggested in his 1931 Glasgow lecture that while the passage grave and gallery grave might not be unrelated in the long run, as far as western Europe was concerned there were two perhaps contemporary traditions, the passage grave found mainly in Iberia and western France, and the gallery grave in the west Mediterranean islands and in southern and non-coastal France.[2]

Applying these principles to Scotland, Childe found passage graves in Orkney, Caithness, Sutherland, and the Hebrides; and gallery graves in the south-west—in Galloway, Arran, Argyll, and also the Hebrides. He thought then that the Caithness tombs were early in the passage-grave series and compared them with tombs in Normandy, Brittany, and southern Spain; he saw their builders spreading up the Atlantic seaways to the Orkneys and from there across to Denmark, definitely rejecting, as did most writers on this subject for many years, Bryce's notion of a dual stream from north-western France. Childe then turned his attention to the gallery graves of south-west Scotland and compared them with the gallery graves of the Pyrenees and Sardinia. He dismissed the idea that the Clyde-Solway gallery graves as he described them could be derived from the Irish or Hebridean passage graves and argued for a west Mediterranean derivation along the Rhône-Garonne route.

These new ideas of Childe's were developed in his *Prehistory of Scotland* published four years after the Glasgow lecture, and here he distinguishes five groups: (i) the long cists as he was then calling them of the south-west, again emphasizing their nearest parallels in the Pyrenees, Catalonia, and Sardinia; (ii) the chambered cairns of Caithness emphasizing the parallels between the corbelled tombs of Caithness and sites like Alcalar, Los Millares, and Palmella; (iii) the collective tombs of the coasts and islands of western Scotland between Loch Etive and Cape Wrath; (iv) the Orkney tombs, most of which he regarded as 'late and specialized variants of the Caithness plan'; (v) the stone circles of Strath Nairn and Strath Spey—the Clava tombs—which he regarded as 'colonists who settled on the Nairn and Spey' by crossing the Moray Firth from eastern

[1] A half-hearted attempt was made to do so for southern Britain by M. C. Burkitt in his *Our Early Ancestors*, Cambridge, 1926, 151.

[2] This suggestion was developed by the present writer in *Proc.Prehist.Soc.*, VII (1941), 1–49.

Sutherland. His summary of all this was, then, that 'it must be concluded, despite all seeming improbabilities, that adventurous voyagers from South France and Portugal did land and settle on the Western and Northern coasts of Scotland respectively'.[1]

Fifteen years after the publication of *The Prehistory of Scotland*, Childe gave another talk to the Glasgow Archaeological Society and surveyed ten years of research on megalithic tombs. He was now prepared to abandon some of his earlier ideas, no longer maintaining, for example, the priority of Scottish passage graves over English and Irish ones, but on the whole he merely strengthened his general position, and it is this that is also set out in books which he wrote in 1940 and 1950.[2] The south-west Scottish gallery graves, together with those from north-eastern Ireland, come from the west Mediterranean and south France—the Corracloona porthole in County Leitrim and the Beacharra ware are now additional arguments, and the passage graves come from Iberia. Childe is now, however, in these later statements much exercised by the fact that so many of the north Scottish passage graves are in long, horned cairns and argues for a hybridization between the long cairn-gallery grave tradition and the passage grave-round mound tradition, either in Scotland itself, or perhaps, he suggests tentatively, in County Sligo.

The most recent and at the same time the most comprehensive statement describing and interpreting the Scottish megalithic tombs is that given by Piggott in his *Neolithic Cultures of the British Isles*, to which reference has already been made. Piggott accepts the dual nature of the megalithic colonization of Scotland, and distinguishes in detail between the Scottish passage graves and gallery graves, but he carries much further than Childe, in ingenious, detailed, and convincing typologies, the idea of hybridization between these two groups. He sees the passage-grave builders settling in the Orkneys and in the Clava area, and also in the Hebrides, and in one or two places in south-west Scotland, and he brings them from Spain and Ireland. He sees the gallery-grave builders settling in south-west Scotland and coming direct from south-west France. By complicated fusions of architectural traditions, he explains the aberrant

[1] *The Prehistory of Scotland*, 59.

[2] The second Glasgow lecture is published in *Trans.Glas.Arch.Soc.*; Childe's *Prehistoric Communities of the British Isles* was published in 1940; his *Prehistoric Migrations in Europe* in 1950. For other statements of his views see *Scottish Geog. Mag.*, 1934, 18–25; *Scotland Before the Scots*, London, 1946; *Prehistoric Scotland* (Historical Association pamphlet 115), London, 1940.

monuments in the Hebrides, Caithness, and the Orkneys.[1] There is little disagreement between Childe and Piggott and it may be said that the Childe-Piggott account of the nature and origins of the Scottish megalithic tombs represents the current, widely accepted, and orthodox view of these splendid monuments. Can we usefully add anything to the extensive literature of description and synthesis which we have surveyed briefly? Is there anything to say but to repeat in slightly different words the doctrine of the dual nature of the Scottish megalithic tombs, the extent of the development in Scotland of secondary megalithic types, and the derivation of the two primary types from the main areas of characterization of these primary types in south-western Europe, the passage grave from Iberia, and the gallery grave from southern France. In one respect at least it seems to the present writer that current Scottish megalithic orthodoxy is questionable, and that is the relation of the Clyde-Solway gallery graves to the gallery graves of southern France. But before we discuss this point of interpretation, let us summarize briefly our existing knowledge of the Scottish megalithic tombs, as that knowledge is presented to us by Childe in *The Prehistory of Scotland* (1935) and *Scotland before the Scots* (1946), by Piggott in his *Neolithic Cultures of the British Isles*, and by the *Inventories* of the Royal Commission of Ancient Monuments in Scotland and excavation reports published in the *Proceedings* of the Society of Antiquaries of Scotland in the last quarter century.

There are upwards of 360 chamber tombs in Scotland, and this figure is to be compared with 250 or thereabouts in England and Wales, probably 1,500 in Ireland and some 6,000 in France. The distribution of these tombs is shown on the map (fig. 7), and it will be seen at once that distributionally these tombs can be divided into five main groups as follows: (1) south-west Scotland, (2) the Western Isles, (3) north-west Scotland, (4) the Orkneys, and (5) the Shetlands. Let us discuss the types of tombs in each of these five groups.

1. South-west Scotland

This group extends from the south end of the Great Glen to the Solway Firth and mainly comprises Argyll, Kintyre, Bute, Arran, Ayr, Wigtown-

---

[1] Special attention should be paid in assessing Piggott's views to Piggott and Powell, *Proc. Soc. Ant. Scot.*, LXXXIII (1948–49), 103–61, and Piggott, 'Excavations in Passage Graves and Ring Cairns of the Clava Group, 1952–3', *Proc. Soc. Ant. Scot.*, LXXXVIII (1954–56), 173–207.

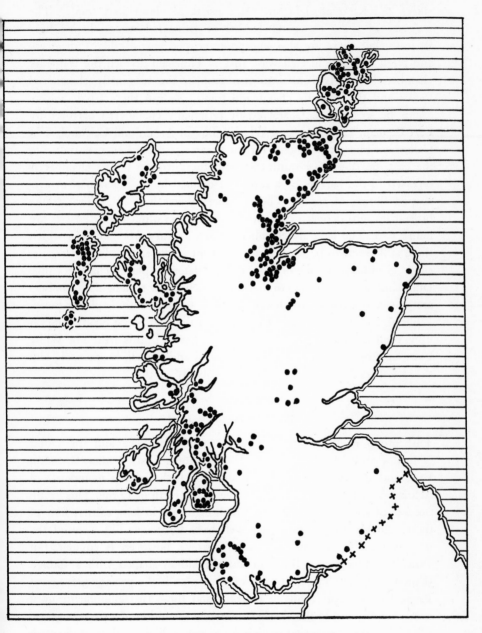

Fig. 7. Chambered Cairns in Scotland.

shire, and Kirkcudbrightshire. It consists of about sixty tombs. The majority of these are parallel-sided or truncated wedge-shaped long barrows, but there are also amorphous-shaped barrows like Cairnderry and High Gillespie in Galloway. Just as Thurnam divided the Wiltshire chambered long barrows into two groups, the terminally chambered tombs and the laterally chambered tombs, so can these Clyde-Solway tombs be so divided. Characteristic terminally chambered barrows are East Bennan, Carn Ban, and Whiting Bay in Arran, and Cairnholy I in Galloway. These monuments for the greater part have their entrance to the east, north-east or south-east, and the entrance to the chamber is recessed in the barrow by a forecourt defined by a semicircular or arc-shaped setting of stones. The chambers themselves are gallery graves broken up into between one and five segments; often the orthostats are imbricated. The laterally chambered barrows vary from some in which there still seems to be some formal element at the east end (perhaps one single chamber) and one or more pairs of laterally placed chambers (like Drannandow in Galloway) to tombs in which single rectangular chambers are scattered around shapeless mounds in an apparently haphazard way. While this is the main part of the story of the south-west Scottish mega-lithic tombs, there are one or two passage graves in this area. The White Cairn at Bargrennan, excavated by Piggott and Powell, is one such, and the chambers on the Water of Deugh probably another.

2. *The Western Isles*

This group comprises the megalithic tombs of Skye and the Outer Hebrides—the islands of Lewis, Harris, North Uist, Benbecula, South Uist, and Barra. In this group should be included the monument of Achnacree at the mouth of Loch Etive in the Firth of Lorne. This group consists of about forty tombs of which eight are in long cairns; four of these, though unexcavated, may well have forecourts like some of the south-west. The normal cairn in this group, however, is circular, but Unival is square, and Rudh'an Dunain kidney-shaped with a funnel-shaped forecourt. The main type of tomb plan is the passage grave as at Barpa Langass and Rudh'an Dunain, and these two monuments most nearly correspond to the classic continental definition of a passage grave. Elsewhere there are sites which look rather like south-west Scottish segmented galleries and a monument like Clettraval in north Uist almost defies classification. Lindsay Scott would have called it a passage grave; the present writer would have at one stage classified it as a gallery grave; Piggott says it 'can only be interpreted as a structural hybrid between the passage grave and Clyde-Carlingford traditions'.[1] This single example of Clettraval shows the difficulty if not the futility of trying to apply a too-rigid classification of megalithic tombs, particularly to what are secondary tomb types in the sense defined by Childe.

3. North-west Scotland

This group comprises Sutherland, Caithness, Easter Ross, Inverness, and Nairn, and includes about a hundred tombs. From the point of view of tomb types they vary very considerably. At the north-east end of the Great Glen, in the valleys of the Beauly, Ness, Nairn, and Spey, to the south side of the Moray Firth are thirty tombs now usually referred to as the Clava group; they are all in round mounds, seven of them contain passage graves like Avielochan and Clava North-East. The remainder, at least twenty sites, consist of a circular enclosure without any passage. To these two types among the Clava tombs Piggott has given the useful names *Balnuaran type* and *Gask* type.[2] North of these Clava tombs from the Great Glen to the Pentland firth are what can usefully be referred to as the Caithness-Cromarty chambered tombs. Some twenty-six of these are in long cairns and Piggott would refer to these as the *Yarrows* type; the remainder, some sixty tombs, are in round mounds which he would describe as *Camster* and derivative types. The long mounds of Yarrows type vary in length from 55 to 240 feet; they are wedge-shaped and have at one end (sometimes at both) semicircular or cuspate forecourts with the ends prolonged into horns—hence the name of 'horned cairns' which has been given to these monuments since the nineteenth century. One unusual monument—Ormiegill in Caithness—is in what can only be described, clumsily, as a short-long or square barrow. These long, horned cairns can be divided into two types in the same way as Thurnam divided the Wiltshire and Cotswold long barrows, and we have divided the south-west Scottish tombs, namely the horned cairns with terminal

---

[1] *Neolithic Cultures*, 225. For Lindsay Scott's views on Clettraval and on Scottish megalithic tombs in general see *Proc. Soc. Ant. Scot.*, LXIX (1934–45), 480–535; *Antiquity*, 1942, 301–6; *Proc. Prehist. Soc.*, 1951, 16–82.

[2] *Neolithic Cultures*, 258–9, and *Proc. Soc. Ant. Scot.*, LXXXVIII (1954–56), 173–207.

chambers like Yarrows itself, and those like Camster I which are laterally chambered. The round mounds of the Camster type vary in diameter from 28 to 75 feet—this latter monument is Camster round itself. All these round mounds cover passage graves. The passage graves in both the Camster and the Yarrows group are unusual; they are corbel-roofed— Camster round is 10 feet high—but are broken up by projecting slabs. These slabs break up the passage as well as the chamber into bays or stalls, and I would like to call the characteristic type of megalithic tomb in the north-east of Scotland the Yarrows-Camster stalled passage grave. Childe would like to call these monuments tripartite passage graves, but it seems to me that the essential peculiarity of them is not merely that the chamber itself is divided along its length into three sections, but that the whole monument is stalled.

4. The Orkneys

There are some forty megalithic tombs in the Orkneys and they display a great variety of plan. The most magnificent tomb is, of course, Maes Howe to which we have already referred; it is a fine passage grave with three side-chambers: other passage graves are Wideford Hill, Cuween, Vinquoy, and probably the Ring of Bookan. Quoyness has a chamber lengthened at right-angles to the passage and has six side-chambers; Quanterness embodies the same idea, but is rectangular in plan. The Holm of Papa Westray, whose discovery by Thomas we have already referred to, has a chamber extended even further at right-angles to the passage, and no less than fourteen side-chambers. All the sites so far mentioned have unimpeded passages and chambers, but there is also in the Orkneys a group of monuments stalled as in the Yarrows-Camster manner. Taversoe Tuack and Unstan are good examples of Orkney stalled passage graves; the stalling exists only in the chamber itself, and these chambers, like the other Orkney passage graves, are T-shaped and have the chamber extended at right-angles to the passage. Blackhammer and Midhowe are remarkable examples of very long stalled chambers. These sites, like the Holm of Papa Westray, are set in unhorned long barrows. The Blackhammer chamber is entered like the Holm of Papa Westray by a short passage from the long side of the mound; Midhowe is entered by a passage from the short end of the long mound.

Two of the Orkney monuments call for special attention. One is

Taversoe Tuack, on Rousay, which Marwick has described as 'after Maes Howe . . . perhaps the most remarkable of all the Orkney cairns'.[1] It was excavated by Grant in 1937 and presents the very unusual phenomenon of two passage graves in one mound placed one above the other, the lower chamber entered from the south-east and the upper from the north-west.[2] The other monument is the Dwarfie Stane on Hoy—a large block of sandstone within which a passage and two side-chambers have been cut. If this is a rock-cut collective tomb, as is widely held, it is almost the only such tomb recognized in north-western Europe, though it is worth remembering that there are rock-cut features in other megalithic tombs, such as Samson 12 in the Isles of Scilly, and that the lower chambers at Taversoe and Huntersquoy are rock cut.[3]

5. The Shetlands

This final group of Scottish tombs comprises sixteen sites in the Shetlands. With one exception these all belong to a type of monument which Bryce, who first studied these tombs in detail, christened 'heel-shaped' cairns. Piggott would divide these into two types, the first, which he calls the *Punds Water* type, consists of a cruciform chamber with a passage opening out a slightly concave façade; these monuments are passage graves in round mounds incorporated in a heel-shaped or oval mound. Piggott's second type is the *Muckle Heog* type; it has the same heel shape, but instead of a passage grave it covers closed cists.[4]

One thing stands out very clearly from a close study of the distribution of the Scottish megalithic tombs; their distribution is basically a coastal and riverine one and can only mean coastal settlements and penetration up the rivers like that from Dornoch Firth up to Loch Shin or up the Spey to Avielochan. We do not really need a wide comparative knowledge of megalithic monuments in Europe as a whole before we can interpret

[1] Hugh Marwick, *Ancient Monuments in Orkney*, Edinburgh, 1952, 15.

[2] On Taversoe Tuack, see W. G. Grant, *Proc. Soc. Ant. Scot.*, LXXIII (1938–39), 155–66. Huntersquoy on Eday is another two-story chamber tomb (*Orkney Inventory*, 56–59).

[3] On the Dwarfie Stane see C. S. T. Calder, *Proc. Soc. Ant. Scot.*, LXX (1935–36), 217–22. The site known as St. Kevin's Bed, Glendalough, in Ireland has been interpreted by Hemp (*Antiquity*, 1937, 348–50) and O'Neil (*Antiquaries Journal*, 1947, 182–3) as another rock-cut collective tomb.

[4] On the Shetland tombs see Bryce, *Proc. Soc. Ant. Scot.*, LXXIV (1939–40), 23–35, and Piggott, *Neolithic Cultures*, 262–3. For the Stanydale 'temple', see below.

the Scottish megalithic tombs: the map alone tells us that their builders are people who came by sea to the isles and coastal plains of Scotland. Often, as Childe first analysed, we can see them settling on raised beach platforms or alluvial gravels adjacent to points of entry on the shore; he noted that on Rousay 'each tomb corresponds to a natural agricultural unit, generally still or till recently farmed by a community and comprising in each case a stream, a strip of good arable land below, and a tract of pasture above the tomb'.[1] The actual settlement sites of the people who buried their dead in the Scottish megalithic tombs are as rare as megalithic settlement sites are in western Europe as a whole. There is a settlement site on the slopes of Wideford Hill just below the passage grave. The potters' kilns of Eilean an Tighe on North Uist excavated by Lindsay Scott may well be those of the Hebridean megalith builders. The settlement site at Rothesay in Bute had pottery such as is found in some of the south-west Scottish collective tombs, but Piggott regards the dominant culture here as of Rinyo-Skara Brae type, which he would classify as Secondary Neolithic. The notion of the Secondary Neolithic Cultures of the British Isles as set out by Piggott is that they represent the acculturation of Neolithic colonists and Mesolithic indigenous hunter-fishers, as Professor Atkinson has discussed (p. 22). Skara Brae on the mainland of Orkney and Rinyo on Rousay, while formally classified as the settlement sites of these Secondary Neolithic people must surely owe something to the megalithic colonists, and it is certainly arguable that the villagers of Skara Brae and Rinyo buried their dead in the Orcadian collective tombs. A vessel in the style described by Lindsay Scott as Rinyo I was found with the latest burials in the Unival chambered tomb in the Hebrides, and the remarkable sherd of pottery from Skara Brae decorated with a design of double spirals and lozenges is in the tradition of the art on the Boyne megalithic tombs.

Our detailed knowledge of the way of life and the material culture of the megalith builders must, however, in the main be drawn from the tombs themselves, that is to say from the material found during excavation, and this information is naturally limited by the amount of excavation that has taken place. About seventy of the 360 Scottish megalithic tombs have been excavated but material remains survive from only forty tombs. The material, apart from pottery, consists of stone axes, leaf-shaped flint arrowheads, plano-convex knives, hollow scrapers, flint knives with

[1] *Scotland Before the Scots*, 34.

polished edges, tranchet arrowheads, cylindrically perforated stone mace-heads, stone discs, and beads of jet and stone. No metal objects have been found in primary burials in any of the Scottish collective tombs, though, as Childe has pointed out, some of the stone types found in Scottish megalithic tombs have been found in Yorkshire associated with bronze weapons in individual graves.[1]

The pottery from the Scottish collective tombs has been studied in detail by Piggott in his *Neolithic Cultures*. We may note the existence of the following main varieties: (1) undecorated round-bottomed bowls of what can most conveniently be called Western Neolithic pottery,[2] (2) undecorated hemispherical bowls with shoulders and concave and flared-out necks which Piggott proposes to call Lyle's Hill ware, (3) decorated carinated bowls with a rim of less diameter than the shoulder and with ornament in shallow channelling or incision, which Piggott would now call Beacharra B ware, (4) much the same kind of pottery, but with the decoration done by impressed twisted or whipped cord such as is not found in the Western Neolithic traditions, and which is Piggott's Beacharra C, (5) shallow open bowls with a vertical collar usually ornamented by channelling or stab-and-drag technique with oblique or horizontal lines, usually referred to as Unstan ware. In addition to these five wares there also occurs some sherds of Beaker, Peterborough, and Rinyo wares, but usually in late primary or secondary circumstances. The amount of Lyle's Hill ware in the Scottish collective tombs is very slight indeed, although it occurs often in the analagous tombs of north-eastern Ireland. It occurred in the blocking of Cairnholy I, but only a single bowl and in the final period of the tombs funerary use; it occurred in the Easterton of Roseisle site in Morayshire, if this is a collective tomb, and there are sporadic finds elsewhere.[3] There is some correlation between the various types of collective tombs and the pottery types; the Beacharra B ware occurs only in south-west Scotland and the Hebrides, and the Unstan ware in the north-east of Scotland and the Orkneys.[4]

The material evidence for the economy of the chambered-tomb

---

[1] *Prehistory of Scotland*, 23.

[2] This includes Piggott's Beacharra A pottery and the undecorated round-bottomed bowls from Orkney, such as the two Unstan pots figured by him in *Neolithic Cultures*, 249.

[3] Callender, *Proc. Soc. Ant. Scot.*, LXIII (1928–29), 29–98; Piggott, *Neolithic Cultures*, 170.

[4] No sherds survive from the Caithness tombs. See Piggott, *Neolithic Cultures*, 248.

builders in Scotland has been well analysed by Childe in his *Scotland before the Scots*. They were, he suggests, mixed farmers who hunted and fished. A typical saddle quern was found in the Rothesay settlement; and an impression of a grain of hulled barley on a sherd from Unstan and of a grain of naked barley on a sherd from Eday. Analogous tombs to the south-west Scottish monuments in Northern Ireland and the Isle of Man have yielded small spelt, emmer wheat and other impressions of *Triticum monococcum-dicoccum* type.[1] The domestic animals include cattle, sheep, pig, and a fairly large number of the cattle bones belonged to immature animals. Professor Watson has noticed this at Skara Brae and said then it was probably due to 'the difficulty of providing winter forage to allow all, or even a large proportion of, the calves to be carried on until the grass grew again in the spring'. Childe argues that hunting played a more important part in the economy of the megalith builders than it did in, say, the villagers of Skara Brae; the animals hunted include red deer, horse and wildfowl. Fish bones and birds' eggs are recorded from Midhowe and shell fish from Yarso and Lower Dunreay.[2]

We now return to the question that much exercised the early writers on Scottish megalithic tombs, and is begged all the time when we talk about the colonization of Scotland by the megalith builders: the question of origins. Where did the megalith builders who settled in Scotland come from? Although in recent years we have moved away from a monogenetic theory for the origin of megalithic monuments in Europe,[3] no one has seriously argued that the Scottish megalithic monuments originated in northern Britain, and most people assume that they represent a movement of people from south-western Europe along the Atlantic seaways from Iberia and France.[4] The question really is by today, Was there one movement or many, and where precisely was the home of these early settlers in Scotland? To attempt an answer we must recollect the catalogue of types of megalithic tomb that have been distinguished in Scotland. Here

[1] K. Jessen and H. Helbaek, *Cereals in Great Britain and Ireland in Prehistoric and Early Historic Times*, K. Danske Vidensk. Selskab, 1944.

[2] For a fuller account of the economy of the collective-tomb builders see Childe, *Scotland Before the Scots*, 34 ff., 'The Megalithic Society'.

[3] Largely as a result of C. A. Becker's reinterpretation of the Danish *dysser*, which has at last removed the difficulties felt by so many in deriving these megalithic tombs from western Europe.

[4] But G. F. Willmot argues for a northern European origin for the megaliths of Britain and France, and on the eastern element in our Neolithic, see Piggott, *Proc. Prehist. Soc.*, 1955, 96–101.

is a minimum list of types that we must distinguish if we are going to engage in any useful discussion of origins: (1) the terminally chambered long barrows of south-west Scotland of the Cairnholy-East Bennan type; (2) the laterally chambered barrows of south-west Scotland; (3) the passage graves of south-west Scotland of the Bargrenan-Water of Deugh type; (4) the passage graves of the Western Isles; (5) the aberrant passage graves or passage grave-gallery grave hybrids of the Western Isles; (6) the Clava passage graves of Piggott's *Balnuaran* type; (7) the Clava tombs of the *Gask* type; (8) the Camster stalled passage graves in round mounds; (9) the Yarrows stalled passage graves in long mounds; (10) the laterally chambered long mounds of north-west Scotland; (11) the Orkney passage graves in the Maes Howe tradition; (12) the Orkney stalled passage graves; (13) the *Punds Water* type of Shetland heel-shaped cairn; and finally (14) the Muckle Heog type of Shetland heel-shaped cairn.

No discussion of the origins of Scottish megalithic tombs can be profitable unless it begins by recognizing the existence of these varieties, and their classification is a matter of objective taxonomy. But is this taxonomy any more than an ingenious academic exercise in nomenclature and classification? Does it mean anything? It begins to look as if it does when we apply, a little more rigidly than he did himself, the principles of interpretation which Childe laid down in his 1931 lecture to the Glasgow Archaeological Society. Let us examine the list of fourteen types in the light of Childe's principle that 'types localized in specific areas will be later inasmuch as they represent regional variants'. Applying this, and remembering the proven example of the succession of lateral- and terminal-chambered long barrows in the Severn-Cotswold region, we can at once remove from the roster of primary megalithic types in Scotland types (2), (5), (8), (9), (10), (12), and (14). Few archaeologists would object to the removal of the laterally chambered types, namely (2), (10), and (14); and probably by now very few the monuments of type (5), which are patently variants and hybrids and part of the secondary development of megalithic architecture in the Western Isles. It might be that a few would cavil still at the removal of types (8), (9), and (12), but it must be emphasized that these monuments have no exact parallels outside northern Scotland; the whole principle of subdividing the chambers into stalls should be regarded as a Scottish development.

We are left then with seven types of Scottish megalithic tombs as representing the possible primary settlement of Scotland, at least on a reasonable basis of argument. These seven types may be conveniently grouped together into four classes posing four separate questions:

(a) the primary Scottish passage graves, namely type (3), (6), and (11)
(b) the primary gallery graves, namely type (1)
(c) the *Gask* type of Clava tomb, i.e. type (7)
(d) the *Punds Water* type of Shetland heel-shaped cairn

Let us deal with the last two questions first. Bryce[1] and Calder[2] have argued for a direct derivation of the Shetland tombs of *Punds Water* type from the Mediterranean. Piggott, while recognizing that these tombs are without parallel in the British Isles, regards the perfectly valid comparisons with Mediterranean types such as Balearic *navetas* and Maltese temples as comparable, but having 'probably no more validity than a recognition of the essential unity of the collective tomb tradition in western Europe where certain ritual elements—chambers, passages, façades, forecourts—recur in various combination in almost every area colonized by the builders of these tombs'.[3] This statement, which I have deliberately quoted in full, and which can be referred to conveniently as the law of the recurring combination of basic features in megalithic tomb architecture, sets out clearly a principle as important and, to all present appearances, as correct as the two principles which Childe adumbrated in his 1931 Glasgow lecture. It is a principle which hardly needs stressing to archaeologists well steeped in the theoretical battles of comparative ethnology, but it does need constant restating to archaeologists who have not learnt the long and repeated lessons of the great anthropological controversies between the diffusionists and the independent inventionists. It is in its essentials the principle that all cultures and all versions of a particular culture have an overall assemblage of traits and that where a culture spreads these traits may crop up in different places and at different times, but that exact and direct connexion between two cultures can only be plausibly argued where there exists the exact reappearance of several linked traits between areas which could be connected, and connected within possible chronological limits. The work of studying megalithic tombs has often been retarded extensively by archaeologists, who with the best will in the world have seized excitedly on only one trait among the

[1] *Proc. Soc. Ant. Soc.*, LXXIV (1939–40), 23–36.
[2] C. S. T. Calder, *Proc. Soc. Ant., Scot.*, LXXXIV (1939–40), 185–205.
[3] *Neolithic Cultures*, 263.

many that may be included in the planning, construction, and use of megalithic tombs, and argued for intercontinental connexions because portholes are found in the Cotswolds, the Paris Basin, and the Deccan, or semicircular forecourts in northern Ireland, northern Scotland, and Sardinia.[1] We perhaps need to state clearly here in the present megalithic context yet another principle supplementary to those of Childe and Piggott and growing out of them, that unless we can show the exact correspondence between several material traits in two distinct areas of megalithic-tomb building we should be very chary of arguing for a genetic relationship between these two areas. This principle, which is the commonplace of sound argument in the diffusion *v.* independent invention controversy, arises here when we discuss the *Punds Water* type of monument. It will arise again when we discuss the other types. Here, as regards the Shetland monuments, the present writer is entirely with the view implicitly expressed by Piggott in the passage quoted from his *Neolithic Cultures of the British Isles.* There is nowhere outside the British Isles where the *Punds Water* type of monument can be exactly paralleled, and it seems to me that we must regard this type and therefore all the Shetland megaliths as local regional developments from traditions already existing in the north of the British Isles.

What of Stanydale, that interesting Shetland monument which we have avoided discussing until now? It was excavated in 1949 by C. S. T. Calder and consists of an oval building with a shallow crescentic forecourt enclosing an area 40 feet by 22 feet, approached by a short passage leading from the crescentic forecourt; the area itself contains six shallow recesses. Two large post holes containing the burnt remains of two spruce posts[2] 10 inches in diameter were found. The structure was almost certainly roofed by a timber ridge roof and probably looked like the conjectural restorations prepared by Mr. Calder. Flat-based pots and sherds of Beaker were found during the excavations. The excavator thought that Stanydale was not a tomb, nor a house, and suggested that it was a religious building, and that the Stanydale temple, as he calls it, was directly related to Mediterranean megalithic architecture. Stanydale,

[1] This is the occupational disease of archaeologists and anthropologists which G. P. Murdock (*Africa: Its Peoples and their Culture History*, 1959, 40–41) calls 'trait-chasing'.

[2] Spruce is not known to be a native tree in Scotland, and it is presumed that the builders of Stanydale used driftwood from North America. See Scott, *Antiquity*, 1951, 151–3.

Calder argues, is 'a temple of Mediterranean lineage'; so pronounced is the resemblance between Mediterranean structures and this Shetland monument that, in his view 'it is almost impossible not to assume that the Maltese temples are the prototypes from which Stanydale is derived and which solve the question of its purpose'.[1] Now, in discussing Calder's interesting views let us be clear on two points: first, there is no inherent reason why there should not be direct contact between the Mediterranean and northern Scotland without leaving any direct trace in between, and secondly, we have probably for very long been too rigidly bound by our terminology of megalithic monuments in calling all the roofed chambered structures tombs. Just as our Christian churches are often full of tombs so it may well be that what we call megalithic tombs were also temples, or that sometimes structures which were initially primarily funerary in purpose later gave rise to monuments that were non-funerary in purpose and function. This is how Professor John Evans has explained the development of the Maltese temples from collective tombs,[2] and it has always seemed to the present writer that some of the great north French gallery graves like Essé and Bournand, and Bagneux, were never functioning tombs,[3] and the same idea is bound to occur when we discuss the Irish monuments that contain central open courts—the lobster-claw tombs of Mahr and the court cairns of R. de Valera. Surely, Piggott was right when he described Stanydale as 'related architecturally to the heel-shaped cairns' of Shetland,[4] and would regard it, in the light of our present comparative knowledge of megalithic monuments, as a local development in Shetland among the people who built the heel-shaped cairns, just as he would regard the court cairns of Ireland as a local development from the Clyde-Carlingford tombs. In both cases the development may have carried with it a change of function.

Our problem of origins is, then, reduced to three questions. Let us now examine the problem of origin of the Clava tombs of Piggott's *Gask* type, the so-called ring cairns. Many writers have regarded these as degenerate examples of the Clava passage graves of *Balnuaran* type; Piggott's recent survey of the Clava tombs shows that the Balnuaran and Gask types are roughly equal in number—there being ten passage graves

[1] *Proc. Soc. Ant. Scot.*, LXXXIV (1949–50), 203 and 205.
[2] *Proc. Prehist. Soc.*, 1953, 41.
[3] *Archaeological Journal*, 1956, 11.
[4] *Neolithic Cultures*, 263.

to nine ring cairns. He argues that the degeneration theory is hard to sustain and quotes the comparison made by the present writer and T. G. E. Powell[1] between the Gask-type tombs and analogous structures in Almeria published by the Leisners.[2] It seems to me that the Gask ring cairns are an integral part of the Clava group of tombs and came to that area of Scotland as part of the movement of settlers who built the Balnuaran type passage graves.

Our problem of origins is then reduced to the two issues of the origin of the passage-grave builders and the origin of the gallery-grave builders. The primary passage graves are those of the Maes Howe type and those of the Balnuaran type. The Bargrenan passage grave in south-west Scotland is probably to be connected, as Piggott and Powell argue, with the undifferentiated passage graves of the Scilly-Tramore group and with the curious tradition that produced monuments like Five Wells in Derbyshire.[3] The Maes Howe type, despite the originality of its architecture, is in plan in the tradition of the cruciform passage graves of the Boyne culture of Ireland, itself ultimately apparented to the passage graves of southern Portugal. It is in this connexion relevant to recollect the spirals on Eday, the oculi ornament on the Holm of Papa Westray, and the lozenges and spirals on the sherd from Skara Brae. The origin of the Balnuaran passage graves of Clava is more complicated; the present writer and T. G. E. Powell suggested that they were among the best examples of primary passage graves in the British Isles;[4] they should be compared with Ile Carn, Les Sept-Iles, La Sergenté, Yvias, Ile Longue, and Barnenez South C and D in Brittany, with Fontenay-le-Marmion in Normandy,[5] and with the classic tombs in the Almerian cemetery of Los Millares and may represent a separate movement of passage-grave builders comparatively early in the general spread of passage graves. Just how this movement took place is another matter; it might have been up the Great Glen, or round the north of Caithness, or possibly up the English Channel from Brittany, Normandy, and so up the east side of England and Scotland. Whichever way it happened it left no comparable colonies on the way.

[1] *Proc. Prehist. Soc.*, 1949, 169–81.

[2] G. and V. Leisner, *Die Megalithgraber der Iberischen Halbinsel,—Der Suden*, 1943, plates 1 to 7.

[3] *Proc. Soc. Ant. Scot.*, LXXXIII (1948–49), 152.

[4] *Proc. Prehist. Soc.*, 1949, 169–87.

[5] Daniel, *The Prehistoric Chamber Tombs of France*, 1960, chapters III and IV, *passim.*

We come now, finally, to the problem of the south-west Scottish gallery graves like East Bennan and Cairnholy and the problem of the origins of these tombs, like the problem of the origin of the Carlingford tombs, strict analogues of the south-west Scottish terminally chambered long barrows, is one about which much has been written in the last twenty years, and violently opposing views held. One school sought the answer in the horned cairns of Sardinia, which admittedly have some points of superficial resemblance to the Clyde-Carlingford tombs, but now that we have fuller knowledge of these Sardinian tombs we see that the resemblances are superficial and can easily and properly be explained according to the law of the recurring combination of basic features, and that in any case none of these Sardinian tombs is early enough to be ancestral to our Scottish and Irish tombs.[1]

Childe and Piggott, as we have seen, see the answer to the origin of the Clyde-Carlingford tombs in southern France. It is perfectly true that here and in Catalonia we get some of the features which recur in different combinations in Scotland; there are segmental slabs breaking up some of the French gallery graves, though La Halliade which is most often cited, is not a happy parallel—it is rather seven megalithic cists set together. There are a few south French collective tombs with semicircular fore-courts; Henri Martin Granel discovered the first on the edge of the Hérault and Gard, and others have been found in Hérault and Gard. They are of two types, first, monuments like Bois Martin with a peculiar and aberrant-shaped megalithic chamber late in the sequence of south French tombs, and secondly utilized natural caves or rather faults in rocks made by karstic erosion, roofed with slabs and preceded by a semicircular setting of stones; a good example of this second type is Ratoul between Montpellier and Ganges.[2] There are, of course, plenty of examples of gallery graves in southern France and many of these are covered in long barrows, sometimes the short-long barrow which appears to have a functional relationship to the long tomb it is covering and sometimes a barrow elongated far beyond structural necessities. This construction of a long barrow for the sake of the barrow, itself now a visible monument

[1] For a modern treatment of the Sardinian material see M. Pallottino, *La Sardegna Nuragica*, Rome, 1950, and Zervos, *La Civilisation de la Sardaigne du début de L'Énéolithique à la fin de la période nouragique*, Paris, 1954.

[2] Martin and Arnal, 'Les Tombes à antennes du Bas Languedoc', *C. R. First Congres d'Etudes Ligures* (1950), Bordighera, 1952 and Pannoux and Arnal, in *Atti Cong. Int. Preistoria e Protohistorica Med.* (1950), 155–78.

of departed friends and relatives, is not a basic feature of the collective burial ritual of the earliest megalith-tomb builders in France, but it becomes so, and both in the passage-grave tradition in north-western France (Barnenez North, Barnenez South, Motte de la Garde, Bougon, Fontenay-le-Marmion) and in the gallery grave-rectangular single chamber tradition we find the growth of the barrow. This importance of the barrow is essential in understanding our British megalithic tombs, because the prehistoric British megalith-builders excelled in building large barrows, from New Grange in Ireland to West Kennet and East Kennet in Wiltshire, and Yarrows and Camster Long in north Scotland.[1] Then, of course, in addition to these features of tomb morphology there does occur in southern France channelled ware which Bryce first compared with the Beacharra B ware,[2] and which comparison has been fruitfully elaborated by Childe,[3] Jacquetta Hawkes,[4] and Piggott.[5]

We can point to no one area, no one group of tombs in southern France where all the features of the Clyde-Solway primary tombs are found. Piggott seems well aware of this when he says that 'it seems impossible . . . to derive the combination of façades, rectangular (sometimes segmented) chambers, and long cairns (sometimes trapezoidal) from any one European source',[6] and so does Hawkes when he proposed in 1940 a fusion of Almerian cist-burials with the passage graves of southern Spain and a spread of these hybrid types via the Catalan-Pyrenean-Basque area to the Clyde-Carlingford area.[7] By today we know the date of the simple rectangular chambers of the Catalan and Basque Pyrenean region[8] makes their role as parents of the Clyde-Carlingford tombs chronologically impossible; they, like the 'dolmens' of Malta and north Portugal are late, not early in the sequence of tomb types.

How can we then resolve this apparent impasse with regard to the origin of the south-west Scottish chambered tombs, which clearly represent, as Childe argued, a primary settlement from outside, and yet seem

[1] On long barrows and gallery graves in southern France see G. E. Daniel, *Ant. Journ.*, 1939, 157; *Proc. Prehist. Soc.*, 1941, 1; (ed) Dickins and Fox, *The Early Cultures of North-West Europe* (1950), 3; *Arch. Journ.*, 1955, 1.

[2] *Proc. Soc. Ant. Scot.*, XXXVI (1901–02), 74–181.

[3] *Arch. Journ.*, 1931, 37–66.

[4] *Arch. Journ.*, 1939, 126–73.

[5] *Neolithic Cultures*, 170 ff.

[6] Piggott, *Neolithic Cultures*, 186–7.

[7] C. F. C. Hawkes, *The Prehistoric Foundations of Europe* (1940), 167.

[8] On this see Pericot, *Los Sepulcros Megalíticos Catalanes y la Cultura Pirenaica*, 1950.

to have no direct continental analogues? I think the answer lies with the earlier antiquaries who stressed the comparison between the horned cairns of Caithness and the monuments of south-west Scotland on the one hand and the horned long barrows of the Cotswolds on the other. We have in the Severn-Cotswold culture of southern Britain a vigorous group of chamber-tomb builders whose first appearance in south Glamorgan, Wiltshire, and Gloucestershire must be surely dated well before 2500 B.C. The tombs of these people can be paralleled in southern Brittany and in the Vendée; here we find long barrows, gallery graves, and gallery graves with pairs of transepts—and it matters nothing in our present context whether, as the present writer has argued, these transepted gallery graves derive from the gallery graves of southern France, or as many others have argued, are forms of passage graves, or perhaps come from types like El Pozuelo in southern Spain.[1] Here, in western France, is a context, culturally and chronologically, that could have given rise to the Severn-Cotswold culture. It seems to me likely that the Severn-Cotswold megalith builders moved from their initial landfall on the shores of the Bristol Channel up St. George's Channel and into the Irish Sea until they reached south-west Scotland and north-east Ireland and eventually the Western Isles of Scotland. We have been accustomed to think of sites like Carn Turne and Pentre Ifan in Pembrokeshire, Trefignath in Anglesey and Capel Garmon in Denbighshire, Ballynamona Lower in County Waterford, and King Orry's Grave and Cashtal yn Ard in the Isle of Man as outlying colonies of the Clyde-Carlingford culture, instead of, as now seems to me likely, stages on the way to the colonization of the north Irish Sea by the Severn-Cotswold builders, who ultimately came from western France. The forecourts at Pentre Ifan and Carn Turne are perhaps intermediate between the Severn-Cotswold forecourts and those of the early Clyde-Carlingford tombs and the façade of West Kennet as revealed by the excavations of a few years ago is in plan closer to Scotland and Ireland than are the cuspate forecourts of some of the Severn-Cotswold tombs. It may well be that the Grey Mare and Her Colts near Portesham on the Dorset coast represents an early stage in what I would now like to call the Severn-Clyde culture. Is it too fanciful to see Breton merchant venturers setting out

---

[1] There are, admittedly no known examples of trapezoid barrows with chambered tombs in them in Brittany, but few chambered mounds in Brittany have been properly excavated. There exist trapezoid unchambered mounds (see S. Piggott, *Antiquity*, 1937, 441).

from the Morbihan and the Loire Atlantique and the Île d'Yeu, having a first landfall in Dorset, then settling on the shores of the Bristol Channel and on to south-west Scotland? At present this seems to me the only working hypothesis to explain the origin of the Clyde-Carlingford culture, in reality an essential part of the chambered long barrow culture of southern England. Of course, this does not mean that the Clyde-Carlingford culture could not have been, or indeed was, in direct contact with southern France or Iberia at some time; how else can we account for Beacharra B ware? But there were many other contacts and their complexity should not obscure what seems to me at present the most likely fact of their origins.[1]

We have, then, in discussing the megalithic settlement of Scotland, various groups of passage-grave builders and one group of gallery-grave builders apparented to the Severn-Cotswold people. When did these colonizing movements take place and how many people did they involve? Scotland gives no direct indication of date in absolute years. We have evidence of comparative date because at Unival, Clettraval and Rudh-an-Dunain the primary (or the initial primary) use of the tombs was pre-Beaker, and the same sort of chronological conclusion can be drawn from the evidence of Nether Largie and Cairnholy I and II. Altogether, of the sites excavated in Scotland that yielded archaeological material eleven had Beakers associated with their latest use. It is clear then, that the megalith builders were well established in western and northern Scotland before the arrival of Beaker-using peoples. For absolute dates we must look to the evidence from France, Ireland, southern Britain, and the Mediterranean in general. It seems likely that some of the Scottish megaliths dated from 2500 B.C. or before, but that the use of some of them went on to the middle of the second millennium B.C. The pumice pendant from Unival described by Scott is in the form of a metal axe; he compared it with the one from the gallery grave of Kerlescan in the Morbihan, but Piggott notes that it is much nearer in shape to the flat metal axes found in the Breton dagger graves which date from 1500–1300 B.C. An overall bracket for the Scottish megalithic tombs of from 2500 to 1300 B.C. would seem to agree with the present evidence. It must not, of course, be thought that each tomb was in use for this long period, though it is not unlikely that any one tomb might have been used for five or six generations. Nor

[1] For discussion of these matters see Daniel, *Proc. Prehist. Soc.*, 1939, 143; *Morgannwg*, 1957, 3; *The Prehistoric Chamber Tombs of France*, 1960.

must it be thought that the tombs represent one movement; Scott argued for successive movements of people extended over perhaps three centuries,[1] and this must surely be so to explain the different groups of passage-grave builders, and the gallery-grave builders with their separate southern French trade connexions.

It is extremely difficult to try to estimate the numbers of people involved in these colonizing movements. J. F. S. Stone has estimated that the total population buried in the south British long barrows is about 1,600,[3] but we have no idea what proportion of chambered tombs have survived from antiquity, nor what section of a community was so interred. The number of individuals found buried in Scottish megalithic tombs varies from one at Corrimony, surviving as stains on the sand surface of the floor[8] to twenty-five in Midhowe, twenty-nine in Yarso, and thirty in Ormiegill. According to Childe's calculations the average for eleven tombs is twelve,[4] but it is interesting that the largest tombs do not necessarily contain the greatest number of individuals. All we can be sure of as we think about the megalithic tombs of Scotland is that the communities that built them were large enough to permit the deployment from time to time of the considerable amount of labour involved in constructing them and heaping large barrows around and on top of them.

We must now turn in conclusion, and briefly, to the stone circles of Scotland, which have not hitherto perhaps received the attention which the megalithic tombs have had. There are very many of them in Scotland, and they fall fairly easily into two categories, those without encircling banks and ditches, and those with such encircling banks and ditches which would in southern Britain be classified as Henge Monuments. The distribution of these two classes of monument is shown on the two maps (figs. 8 and 9).

Many of the first class of monument surround a central burial which may be marked by a barrow; but more often there is just a central cist such as the sites excavated on Arran by Bryce.[5] They vary in diameter from 17 feet to 45 feet, and some of the stones are as much as 10 feet high. Most are single circles, but one on Mauchrie Moor consisted of two, and

[1] *Proc. Soc. Ant. Scot.*, LXXXV (1950–51), 18.

[2] *Wessex Before the Celts* (London), 1958, 51.

[3] Piggott, *Proc.Soc.Ant.Scot.*, LXXXVIII (1954–56), 182–3.

[4] *Scotland Before the Scots*, 37.

[5] *Proc. Soc. Ant. Scot.*, IV, (1954), 499; *Book of Arran*, 113.

there may have been a twin circle encircling a barrow at Newbridge west of Edinburgh.[1] The date of these unembanked stone circles ranges from 1700 to 1800 B.C. through to 1000 B.C.; the graves associated with them have yielded pottery from Food Vessels to Cinerary Urns.

The second class of stone circle, the henge monuments, were studied by J. G. D. Clark when publishing his excavations at Arminghall in Norfolk,[2] and later by R. J. C. Atkinson in publishing the Dorchester (Oxfordshire) monuments.[3] Clark listed three sites in Scotland—the Ring of Brodgar and the Ring of Stennis in Orkney and the Broomend of Crichie site in Aberdeenshire. To these three sites Atkinson was able to add another four, namely Overhowden, Oxton, Berwickshire, recognised by S. and C. M. Piggott as a henge monument in 1949; Cairnpapple, excavated by Piggott in 1947–48; Ballymeanoch, Argyll, excavated by Greenwell in 1864, and the Broadlee Middlebie, Dumfrieshire, discovered by Dr. J. K. S. St.Joseph by air photography in 1947. To this list four more monuments have recently been added, all in Easter Ross.[4]

In 1939 S. and C. M. Piggott suggested that the henge monuments should be divided into two classes, those like Mayburgh and Arminghall with only one entrance and those like Arbor Low and the Bull Ring with two.[5] Atkinson developed this classification and suggested tentatively that what he called his Class I (the single-entrance monuments) were an element of the Neolithic Culture of Great Britain and more particularly the Secondary Neolithic Cultures, while the double-entrance or Class II monuments he tentatively ascribed to the A-C Beaker culture. In Scotland, Overhowden, Conbridge, Contin, and Culbokie belong to Class I, while the others to Class II. But it cannot be pretended that at the present moment we know a great deal about the unembanked and embanked stone circles of Scotland; certainly the stone-circle builders showed the same individuality and versatility as did the Scottish megalith tomb builders. The recumbent stone circles of north-east Scotland may be, as has often been suggested, in some way related to the earlier standing circles; and

---

[1] *Inventory of Midlothian*, no. 131.

[2] *Proc. Prehist. Soc.*, 1936, 1.

[3] 'The Henge Monuments of Great Britain', in Atkinson, C. M. Piggott, and N. K. Sandars, *Excavations at Dorchester, Oxon.*, Oxford, 1951.

[4] A. A. Woodham, *Proc. Soc. Ant. Scot.*, LXXXVII (1952–53), 72–79. Additional sites have since been identified by the Royal Commission on Ancient Monuments (Scotland) and added to the map, fig. 9.

[5] *Antiquity*, 1939, 140.

Fig. 8. Stone Circles (unembanked).

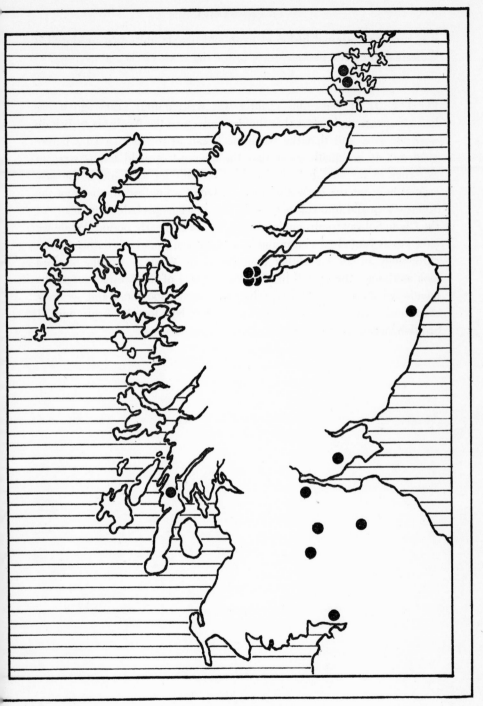

Fig. 9. Henge Monuments.

it is surely an original fusion of tomb and temple ideas that produced at Callernish the little passage grave inside the stone circle and avenues.

POSTSCRIPT: Since this chapter was written four years ago it has become increasingly clear that the dates given to the Neolithic in Britain were too late, and that the Neolithic began in the British Isles before 3000 B.C. It is equally clear that the Severn-Cotswold tombs were in existence in the first half of the third millennium B.C., and if the case argued here for the derivation of the Clyde-Carlingford tombs from the Severn-Cotswold tombs is accepted, then it seems probable that many of the Clyde-Solway tombs might also date from this early period. While we have not as yet (1962) a clear and certain pattern from C 14 dating for the chronology of all megalithic monuments in Western Europe it does look as though the overall bracket for the date of the Scottish megaliths mentioned above should be perhaps '2700 to 1300 B.C.', and we may even find that a date of 2700 B.C. is too late for the beginning of Scottish megalithic architecture.

CHAPTER THREE

Traders and Metal-workers

At the beginning of the second millennium B.C. we have in Scotland a number of population groups whose economy was basically that of stone-using agriculturalists, with a surviving element of hunting and food-gathering tradition. The archaeological evidence for these communities has been surveyed in the foregoing chapters: settlements such as those in Orkney, and indicated by pottery or stone finds elsewhere; ceremonial monuments of the 'Henge' type; and above all the collective chambered tombs. We have seen the diverse strains which contributed to this amalgam of peoples, ranging from the surviving inhabitants technologically in a Mesolithic state of culture, to the varied immigrant groups colonizing Scotland from farther south in Britain, or coming from overseas by way of the western approaches. A certain duality of settlement-pattern has become apparent, with the builders of chambered tombs in the west and north, and the peoples who are archaeologically represented by the Secondary Neolithic cultures, together with other groups not using the chambered tomb rite, in the east and south-east. Whatever the origins of these last, however, the main weight of colonization in the cultures we have been discussing seems certainly to have been on the western and northern shores and islands of Scotland.

Overlapping with at least the continued use of collective chambered tombs, if not of their building, and almost certainly contemporary in part with the Secondary Neolithic Cultures in Scotland, was a phase of immigration and settlement of wholly different origin. In these same early centuries of the second millennium B.C. there impinged on the eastern coasts of Britain a complex of immigrant movements whose origins, broadly speaking, lay in the Rhineland, the Low Countries, and the North European plain. As we have seen, certain elements in our British Neolithic Cultures of the Windmill Hill group may well have had origins in much the same area, and the arrival of the Beaker-using Cultures and their congeners with which we now have to deal, may indicate a renewing and intensification of contacts across the North Sea rather than a wholly novel event. However this may be, with the colonization of Britain by the Beaker people, we enter into a new phase in our prehistory. For the next millennium or so the British Isles, though never without their contacts along the western seaways, are dependent mainly on central Europe for technological innovations, trade, and the interchange of ideas. But it is probably to trade connexions westwards of the Rhine that we have to look for the remarkable and short-lived phase in the middle of the second millennium B.C. when Britain and the Mediterranean seem to have been in close and memorable contact.

The process of immigration and colonization in early second millennium Scotland has been considered by more than one archaeologist, notably by Childe in 1935 and 1946,[1] and by Lindsay Scott in 1951.[2] Scott's paper differs from other treatments of the subject in that he attempted to survey as a single whole the complex movements of a millennium without what appeared to him to be an artificial distinction into those attributable to 'Neolithic' or to 'Early Bronze Age' Cultures. This approach has its value, and Scott's treatment of the geographical background in its relationship to movements of trade and migration, and his discussion of the sources of the raw materials needed by the communities in question, form a notable contribution to our understanding of the problems involved.

But much of the argument in his paper is vitiated by a curious bias towards a western derivation for almost all the significant archaeological traits under discussion: the cist burial common among Beaker-using communities in north Britain is attributed to a Breton or Iberian origin, and certain of the Scottish Beakers are again referred to Breton prototypes. Both these points are discussed below, and for the present one may merely

[1] *The Prehistory of Scotland* (1935), *Scotland Before the Scots* (1946).
[2] 'The Colonisation of Scotland in the Second Millennium B.C.', *Proc. Prehist. Soc.*, XVII (1951), 16–82.

plead for a recognition of the inevitable complexity of primitive folk-movements, and of the nature of the archaeological evidence from which those under discussion are inferred, which not infrequently calls for a frank statement of ignorance rather than the contrivance of a deceptively neat pattern of wholesale derivation from one or other region of Europe.

One distinctive cultural trait does, however, stand out, dividing the makers of chambered tombs from the Beaker-using immigrants, and that is the rite of single-grave burial characteristic of the latter. The tradition of collective burial in a tomb to which recurrent access can be gained by the members of the family or group entitled to use it is wholly distinct from the rite of burying a person in an individual grave, even if (as on occasion) more than one such single grave is included below a common cairn or mound, or forms part of a regular cemetery. This single-grave rite in the British Isles unites a variety of traditions expressed archaeologically by differences of pottery or other grave-goods, and once established continues, whether as inhumation or cremation burial, throughout our prehistory. In our ensuing study of the peoples of Scotland in the second millennium B.C. we have to deal almost exclusively with the evidence from graves, supplemented by stray finds of the copper or bronze tools and weapons which come increasingly into use during this period.

The earliest of our single-grave colonists are, as we shall see, those who made certain characteristic forms of pottery vessels known as Beakers, and they have a particular Scottish interest in that they formed the subject-matter of the original studies in the Bronze Age pottery of the British Isles made at the beginning of this century by that notable Scottish archaeologist, Lord Abercromby. His views on Beakers, published in 1912, have, with certain important modifications, been in the main accepted doctrine among British and Continental archaeologists since his day.[1] But there are certain fundamental assumptions in Abercromby's thesis which have never been critically examined, and these have particular bearing on the problems of the Beaker colonization of Scotland.

Abercromby's overwhelming contribution to British archaeological thought was that, recognising and demonstrating the close affinities between pottery of the Beaker type in Britain and on the Continent, he went on to infer that its appearance in this country could only be accounted for by assuming an actual 'invasion' or immigration of peoples accustomed to make such pots, probably from the Rhineland and the

[1] *Bronze Age Pottery, passim*, esp. I, chaps. v–vi; II, chap. xii.

Low Countries, to these shores. This concept of circumstances obtaining in European prehistory analogous to and not dissimilar from those of earlier historic times, revolutionary at the beginning of this century, has, of course, now become a commonplace, but its originality as conceived and presented by Abercromby must not be forgotten. He, too, was original (but not alone) in stressing the importance of pottery as an index to cultural change or movement of peoples in prehistory, and it is sometimes forgotten that his great book was a study, not of the British Bronze Age, but only of its pottery. Oversanguine of the potentialities of his new approach, he thought that the typology of pots and their ornament was a sure guide to actual folk-movement, and even to an absolute chronology.

From the nineteenth-century archaeologist John Thurnam, Abercromby took over a typological classification of British Beaker pottery into three classes, A, B, and C, of which he seems to have regarded A as the vessel characteristic of an initial landing of a small number of colonists from the Continent, 'probably somewhere on the coast of Kent'.[1] He is nowhere specific about the relationship to such vessels of his Type B, though he implies that some of the latter may have been made by the primary invaders, too. But Type C he considered to be an insular degeneration from Type A, developing during the slow northward progress, from Kent to Caithness, of people making Beakers and inexorably moving north at the rate of 'about fifty miles in every generation'.[2]

In 1929–31 Childe, Grimes, and Clark[3] pointed out that in fact the British as well as the Continental evidence pointed to the priority of the B type of Beaker over A, but the relationship between Types A and C was accepted in the same terms as set out by Abercromby: Scotland, with a certain number of Type B Beakers and an overwhelming majority of Type C, would on this showing have been very largely a province colonized at a late stage by descendants of the makers of Type A vessels. In 1934, however, Margaret Crichton Mitchell found it necessary, as the result of a detailed study of the Scottish Beaker pottery, to suggest that Abercromby's views were invalid, and that the close correspondence in ornament between Scottish and Continental vessels indicated that 'Aberdeen-

[1] *ibid.*, II, 111.
[2] *ibid.*, *loc. cit.* and I, 85.
[3] Childe, *Danube in Prehistory* (1929), 200–1; Grimes, *Proc. Prehist. Soc. E. Anglia*, VI (1931), 347; Clark, *Ant.*, V (1931), 415.

shire has undoubtedly been colonized from Holland and the Rhineland'—
a view based very largely on an analysis of Type C Beakers, on accepted
doctrine derivatives from Type A within Britain. She still felt that Type C
Beakers were derivative forms, not only of Type A but of Type B as well,
but saw that Abercromby's hypothesis of a single landing-place for the
original immigrants was untenable, and considered that 'the whole of the
east coast of Britain from the Thames to the Dee was subjected to a series
of incursions'.[1]

These views were cautiously endorsed by Childe in 1935,[2] but their
full implication does not seem to have been appreciated. If one considers
the evidence afresh, however, the inevitable conclusion is that Abercromby's A–C sequence must be reversed, and the C Type (or Short-
Necked) Beakers regarded as the products of immigration from the Low
Countries direct to north Britain, with the subsequent development of
Type A (or Long-Necked) Beakers in Britain as an insular variant. For one
cannot escape the fact, often evaded or ignored, that these Type A
Beakers have no true Continental prototypes which will satisfactorily
account for all their features.

Our knowledge of the Bell-Beaker cultures of Europe has been greatly
clarified by recent studies. The general picture now presented is an
Iberian origin for Bell Beakers, and a subsequent rapid spread from the
coastal regions of Spain and Portugal into the western Mediterranean, up
the Atlantic coast of France, into the Rhineland and the Low Countries,
and by uncertain routes into Central Europe. In these new centres, the
original Beaker types became characteristically modified by contact with
local late Neolithic cultures, and there then followed a widespread
movement of reflux westwards, whereby the modified types of Bell
Beaker were carried back even as far as the original Iberian homeland.
The Bell-Beaker colonization of Britain was part of this Reflux Movement:
practically no evidence exists for real contacts in the primary phase of
maritime expansion from the west.[3] As a result of the reassessment of the
Dutch evidence by van der Waals and Glasbergen,[4] we can come nearer

[1] *Proc. Soc. Ant. Scot.*, LXVIII (1933–34), 132–88, esp. 134, 161.
[2] *Prehist. Scot.*, 85, 87.
[3] Sangmeister, *Zephyrus* VIII (1957), 257; XI (1960), 131, and in Junghans
et. al., *Metallanalysen kupferzeitliche und frühbronzezeitliche Bodenfunde aus Europa*
(1960); Maluquer de Motes, *Zephyrus* XI (1960), 119; Piggott in *Culture and
Environment: Essays in Honour of Sir Cyril Fox*.
[4] *Palaeohistoria*, IV (1955), 5–46.

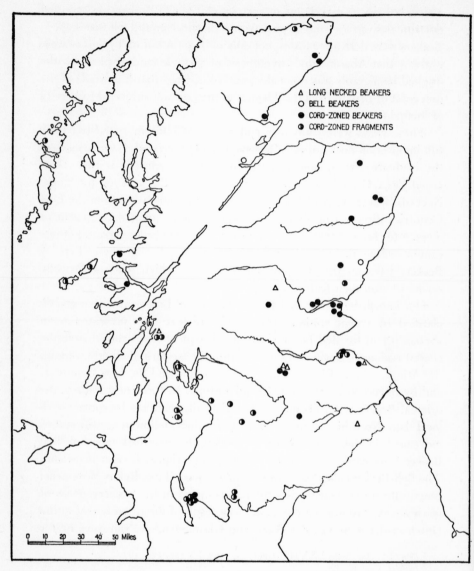

Fig. 10. Distribution of Long-Necked Beakers, Bell Beakers and Cord-zoned Beakers in Scotland (By Miss R. Crawford).

to understanding the Scottish situation so far as the pottery types are concerned. As we shall see, other elements, such as grave-types and certain stone implements, raise problems still difficult of resolution.

In addition to the general resemblances in the decorative schemes of many of the Scottish Short-Necked Beakers and those of Holland, striking resemblances exist between vessels as a whole. Margaret Mitchell noted, for instance, how a Beaker from Oostereng in Holland 'could easily be mistaken for a typical Morayshire example',[1] and again the resemblance between another more recently published Dutch Beaker, from Ermelo,[2] and one from Edzel in Angus,[3] is extremely striking (Pl. 6). Such examples, added to the less precise, but statistically more significant, details of ornament and form common in a large series of vessels from the two regions, leave one in little doubt that the Scottish and north English Short-Necked Beakers represent a component in the complex of the Beaker immigrations into Britain having direct affiliations with the Netherlands.

The recent study of the Dutch Beaker types just mentioned enables us to define this relationship with more precision. In Holland, as elsewhere in north and central Europe, we have to deal with two main strains contributing to the ceramic traditions under discussion, those deriving from the Bell-Beaker Cultures and those from the central and northern European Corded-Ware groups. So far as our Short-Necked Beakers are concerned, we are dealing with developments within the Bell-Beaker series, which in Holland take the form of a move away from the smooth S-curve of the Bell-Beaker prototype towards an angularity of profile and (in its final Dutch form) a broadening of the vessel in proportion to its height. It is in the transitional forms—in the new classification Type 2^{1c}— between the true Bell-Beakers (Types 2^{1a} and 2^{1b}) and the developed Veluwe Type (2^{1d-f}) that we find the close parallels to the Scottish Short-Necked Beakers already noted: the Veluwe Beakers are, in fact, parallel developments within the Netherlands to our Long-Necked (Type A) Beakers in Britain, both variants emphasizing the angular neck of the vessel, though each in its own local version. It looks therefore as if the main component in our British Short-Necked Beakers was provided by an emigration from the Netherlands to Britain at a point in the development of Dutch Beaker types just before the emergence of the Veluwe variants:

[1] loc. cit., 159; Oostereng Beaker in Oudheid. Meded., XIV (1933), Taf. II, 8.
[2] Abercromby, no. 242; Mitchell, no. 74.
[3] Bericht Rijkdienst. Oudheid. Bodem. Nederland, V (1954), Pl. XI, Afb. 2.

contributions from other adjacent regions such as the Rhineland are not, however, excluded.

When we turn to the Scottish Beakers of Abercromby's Type B we find that they are in fact divisible into two main groups, which again reflect Continental classifications. Abercromby had indeed distinguished Types B1 and B2, and the present writer emphasized the validity of this division in 1938,[1] but of these two variants, only B1 occurs in Scotland. But Childe in 1946 had pointed out a third sub-type, which he named B3, and such vessels have, in fact, a predominantly Scottish and north English distribution in these islands.[2] It is convenient to denote these two types by descriptive names—Bell-Beakers (B1) and Cord-Zoned Beakers (B3), since the former come closest to the Continental Bell-Beaker series, and the latter are covered with fine impressed cord lines in horizontal zones from rim to foot.

Scottish Bell-Beakers of Abercromby's B1 class are, in fact, very rare, but are in general of forms which could be paralleled as well or better in the Rhineland than in Holland. In both these Continental regions the characteristic feature of a few lines of impressed cord immediately inside the lip of the vessel, not uncommon in Scotland, appears: this links the types with the Corded-Ware traditions already mentioned as forming a component in the Dutch series, and such Beakers would compare with the Type 2^{11a} series of van der Waals and Glasbergen. The suggestion has more than once been made that some of the British Bell-Beakers were of Breton derivation, and Lindsay Scott also attributed to such a source the Scottish Cord-Zoned Beakers to be discussed below, but the Corded-Ware elements present in almost all our Bell-Beakers shows that they must have a Rhenish or Dutch origin.

The Dutch equivalents of our Cord-Zoned Beakers (Type 2^{11b}) are themselves members of a group with a fairly restricted distribution between the Rivers Elbe and Meuse, and in the Rhineland as far south as Mainz.[3] Beakers of this type are sporadically scattered in west France from Brittany to the Charente and the western Pyrenees, and their presence in these regions gave rise to Scott's hypothesis of a west French derivation for the Scottish examples, but, as we have seen, in both instances we must be

[1] *Proc. Prehist. Soc.*, IV (1938), 56.

[2] *Actas y Mem. Soc. Espan. Antrop. Ethno. y Prehist.*, XXI (1946), 169.

[3] Van der Waals and Glasbergen, *loc. cit.*; Struve, *Einzelgrabkultur in Schleswig-Holstein* (1955), Taf. 36.

dealing with the Reflux Movement of trade and colonization westwards from Rhenish, Dutch or North German starting-points. In Scotland, these Cord-Zoned Beakers are especially characteristic of settlement sites in coastal sand-dune areas such as Luce Bay in Galloway or Gullane in East Lothian.

On the pottery evidence alone, then, we have reason to believe that Scotland was receiving immigrants, at the beginning of the second millennium B.C., from a region or regions between the mouth of the Elbe and that of the Rhine and Meuse. The Short-Necked Beakers have their closest affinities with the Dutch derivatives of Bell-Beakers at the stage immediately antecedent to the local development there of the Veluwe Type: if the radio-carbon dates for certain Dutch Beaker finds be accepted, this stage would date to *c.* 1700 B.C. The Bell-Beaker and Cord-Zoned types would on the Dutch evidence be rather earlier, perhaps by one or two centuries, the Cord-Zoned Beakers having radio-carbon dates of 1980±70 B.C. and 2145±110 B.C. in Holland and north Germany respectively, while one in Yorkshire has a date of 1795±150 B.C. What precipitated these movements of population, we cannot say, but it is possible that we should think in terms of natural events such as accelerated coastal erosion and marine inundations. Flooding of this kind is known to have occurred rather later in the north European Beaker sequence in the valleys of the Lower Elbe and the Bille as well as on our own south-eastern shores.

It is usual to associate the Beaker Cultures of Britain with the beginnings of metallurgy in copper, bronze, and gold. But, in fact, the correlation is by no means so close as is often assumed, and so far as Scotland is concerned we may note that of some 380 finds of Beakers, almost wholly from graves, in only two instances, and a probable third, were the pots associated with copper or bronze objects. At Cairn Greg, Linlathen, Angus, a riveted flat knife-dagger was found with a Beaker burial; fragments of a tanged-and-riveted dagger were in the Glenforsa burial in Mull, and at Crawfurd in Lanarkshire a bronze arm-ring accompanied a beaker.[1] It will be more convenient to discuss these metal objects with others of similar type at a later stage.

In four Scottish Beaker graves were found stone bracers or archers' wrist-guards,[2] and in eight, one or more barbed-and-stemmed flint arrowheads.[3] These associations of archers' equipment with Beakers are

---

[1] Mitchell, nos. 77, 89–90, 228.

[2] Nos. 8–9, 89–90, 356; *Proc. Soc. Ant. Scot.*, LXX (1935–36), 326.

[3] Nos. 8–9, 10–11, 21, 25, 26, 119, 193; *Proc. Soc. Ant. Scot., loc. cit.*

well known elsewhere, both in England and on the Continent, but it is of interest to note that whereas in England the associations of bracers (and usually of arrowheads) are with Bell-Beakers, the Scottish graves under consideration contained Short-Necked Beakers. This suggests a likelihood of contemporaneity, and of common traditions, between the two groups concerned. The Scottish bracers (seven in all) are, of central European four-hole types, except for two of the more widely dispersed two-hole type, known also in Iberia. The equipment of the Scottish Beaker people as reflected in their graves is therefore virtually Neolithic, and a stone and a flint axe from a couple of graves emphasize this fact.[1]

There are two further points in connexion with the makers of Beakers in Scotland, and the first is the physical type of the people. The skeletons from the Scottish graves, like those elsewhere in Britain associated with Beaker pottery, are consistently of a type distinct from those of the collective-chambered tombs, and if nothing else indicated the advent of a new element in the population, the skeletal remains would indicate such an event. We encounter a population taller and more heavily built than the chambered-tomb builders—an average male stature of 5 feet 9 inches as against 5 feet 6 inches for Scotland—and with a broader face and shorter skull. The Scottish skulls show a slight but significant variation from those of England, those north European traits classed as 'Borreby' and 'Corded' by Coon being hardly perceptible, but in general the British skull types are closely allied to those of the Beaker Cultures in the Rhineland, Moravia, and Austria.[2]

The predominant type of single-grave burial in Scotland, whether accompanied by a Beaker, a Food Vessel, by other grave-goods or none at all, is in a slab-lined rectangular pit with cover-stone, or cist. Less frequent are pit graves without a stone lining and cover; still less common are such burials under a barrow or cairn, but one must remember that small barrows could easily be destroyed by ploughing in those areas of heavy agricultural exploitation in east Scotland where so many Beaker and Food-Vessel burials occur. This state of affairs is not confined to the present political boundaries of Scotland, but continues southwards across the Border to a point approximating to the latitude of the River Tees.

[1] Nos. 8–9, 21.
[2] Coon, *Races of Europe* (1939), 157 ff., cf. Brothwell, *Advancement of Science*, March 1960, 311–22.

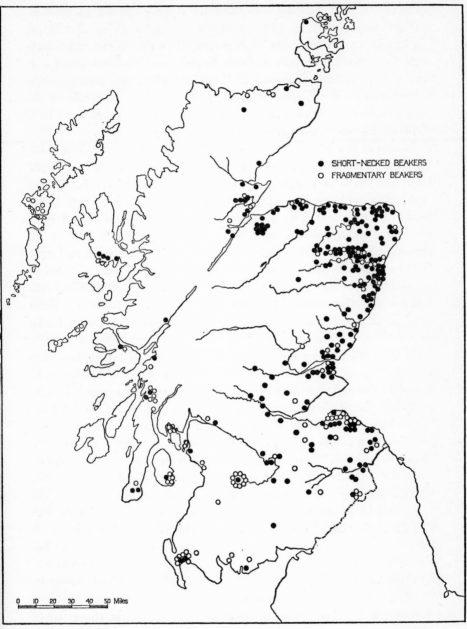

Fig. 11. Distribution of Short-Necked Beakers and fragments of Beakers in
Scotland (By Miss R. Crawford).

South of this line, early second millennium single-grave inhumations are normally beneath a large cairn or barrow, exceptionally in cists or pit graves without or with a very small mound. Normally, in fact, the burials with Short-Necked Beakers in north England and Scotland are in cist graves. This duality in grave-form, with what on linguistic analogy might be called an 'isotaph' approximately on the northern boundary of the county of York, is more appropriately discussed later on, when we have considered other Scottish graves of the same types.

In four or five inhumation graves, at least three of them under a cairn, the skeleton was accompanied by a stone shaft-hole battle-axe of a simple form, with flat or very slightly concave upper and lower faces. Battle-axes of this type have been found in four English graves associated with Long-Necked Beakers, and in several instances with large riveted knife-daggers which analysis suggests are normally of bronze rather than copper: in all, some twenty graves with such battle-axes are known in Britain, and stray finds are relatively numerous. The foreign affinities of such weapons of prestige are to be found in the Corded Ware and related cultures in North Europe, and their association with barrow or cairn burial is almost constant. Their presence in Britain must be related to the same burial rite, with its dominance south of the River Tees, and their comparative rarity in Scotland is in accord with the dominance of burial there in a simple cist or pit grave, and perhaps, too, with the rarity of Corded Ware physical traits perceived by Coon in the skeletal series. In general it looks as though the predominance of large barrows in England south of the Tees is to be related to the presence of battle-axes, and to indicate a population element in this region only thinly represented north of the 'isotaph' already mentioned. The use of bronze and other factors combine to demonstrate the comparatively late date of such graves, roughly contemporary with the first phase of the Wessex Culture mentioned below.

It must be admitted that such a thesis does not account for the fact that the normal burial rite of the Dutch Beaker people is beneath a small barrow, and cists of the north British type are virtually unknown in that region. Such cists do occur, however, sporadically in northern Europe as an alternative to a simple pit grave,[1] and it should be stressed that structurally a cist is a stone lining to a grave, and may represent nothing more than an alternative to a lining or coffin of wood. The remarkable group of massive cists in the Crinan region of Argyll with the end-slabs let into

[1] e.g. in the Saale region: Fischer, *Gräber der Steinzeit im Saalegebiet* (1956).

grooves in the side stones strongly suggest a reminiscence of carpenters' techniques transferred to stone. Cist burial, in fact, seems to be a form of grave which can recur in many places and at many times without the necessity of assuming any direct connexions between its different manifestations, and small barrows may easily be obliterated.

The last group of inhumation burials we have to note in Scotland is that characterized by the presence of a pottery vessel of the Food-Vessel type, sometimes accompanied also by a jet or lignite space-plate necklace, sometimes with the necklace alone present with the skeleton. Food Vessels constitute a crux in British prehistory, for despite ingenious attempts to provide prototypes for their forms in Continental Europe, it must be admitted that, although partial analogues for certain features might be found in the pottery of certain cultures of the north European plain, as a whole the Food Vessels of the British Isles represent an insular phenomenon. It seems possible that the 'vase' and 'bowl' series are, in fact, the extreme poles of a continuous typological sequence, and that we need not think we have to deal with two disparate elements. In Scotland, rather over three-quarters of the burials with Food Vessels are by inhumation, the remainder by cremation; like Beaker burials they are normally in cist graves, exceptionally under a mound, and the River Tees isotaph applies to Food Vessel burials as well as to others. A classification can be made which distinguishes English from Irish influences in the Scottish Food vessels, and also recognizes the development of local types. Where the physical type of the skeletons found with such pottery has been determined, it appears to be indistinguishable from that associated with Beaker burials in the same region. A final point is that virtually no instance of demonstrably male equipment with a Food Vessel burial is known, whereas the necklaces already mentioned, and the small plano-convex flint knives also found with burials of this type do suggest the burials of females.

To anticipate a point argued at greater length later on, the time range for Food Vessels and for jet space-plate necklaces appears to spread from a probable overlap with Beakers to a date after the establishment of the Wessex Culture in the south of England: there is a case for equating some of the 'bowl' Food Vessels with the Montelius III phase of the Northern Bronze Age, and consequently with a date after 1200 B.C. It is tempting, but unproven, to think of the Food Vessel in north Britain as originating as a 'native' counterpart of the exotic Beaker, and being the vessel appropriate to a woman's grave. Later, the custom of making Beakers (or

at least, of placing them with the dead) may have given way to the ubiqui-
tous use of the Food Vessel as the funerary accompaniment.

The Henge Monuments, originating in Secondary Neolithic contexts,
have already been mentioned in earlier chapters. The double-entrance type
has some claims to be related to the makers of Beakers, and the unique site
on Cairnpapple Hill deserves mention here as providing a remarkable
stratified sequence through the first half of the second millennium B.C.[1]
Here a cremation cemetery with ritual pits of Secondary Neolithic type
(Cairnpapple I) was succeeded by a double-entrance Henge of standing
stones within a bank and ditch, associated with Beaker burials (II). This
structure was then dismantled, and a cairn containing a cist burial with
an inhumation with a Food Vessel was built on the site (III); later this
cairn was enlarged to twice its size to contain two burials by cremation in
Cinerary Urns of types to be discussed later on, one with a ring-headed
bone pin which can be approximately dated to a position contemporary
with the later phase of the Wessex Culture, in the fifteenth century B.C. (IV).

As will have been seen, with the exception of the Henge Monuments
and settlements attested by scattered sherds in sand-dunes, our early
second millennium prehistory has so far been reconstructed from grave-
archaeology. But side by side with this we have to consider another body
of evidence, that of tools and weapons of copper or bronze, and ornaments
of gold. For technologically we are now in the British Early Bronze Age,
and a number of most interesting problems arise when we have to consider
the beginnings of metallurgy in Scotland, and in the British Isles as a
whole.

The adoption of a metal-using technology by peoples formerly accustomed to use stone for their edge-tools is an affair of some complexity,
involving considerable knowledge of a more than rudimentary field
geology in ore-prospecting, together with a familiarity with the tricky
techniques of metal smelting and working. So far as the British Isles are
concerned, it is usually thought that the technical skills involved were
brought by craftsmen associated with the Beaker immigrations already
discussed, and that they represent a northwesterly extension of Central
European metallurgical traditions. On the other hand, an existence of an
equally early school of copper-working in Ireland and perhaps west
Britain, owing nothing to central Europe but derived from Iberia, has
often been claimed, but it is difficult to substantiate except on *a priori*

[1] *Proc. Soc. Ant. Scot.*, LXXXII (1947–48), 68–123.

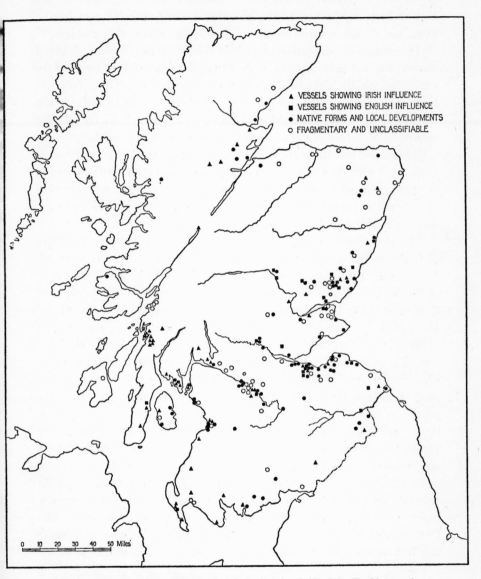

Fig. 12. Distribution of Food Vessels in Scotland (By Mr. D. Simpson).

grounds. The systematic analysis of copper and bronze objects of the Early Bronze Age in the British Isles and on the Continent, now in progress, has already contributed materially toward solving this problem.[1]

The natural circumstances of geology render the distribution of natural copper, tin, and gold deposits in the British Isles beyond the range of the territories initially colonized by the Beaker immigrants. Tin is found in Cornwall alone; copper and gold are notably abundant in Ireland, but also occur in Wales, north-west England, and Scotland. So far as early metallurgy in Scotland was concerned, copper and gold could be obtained from local sources; tin as elsewhere involved trade either with south-west England or with the Continent. But when one looks at the distribution, in Scotland itself, of the metal sources in relation to the distribution-pattern of the earliest copper and bronze objects, and of both in relation to the areas of Beaker settlement, one sees curious disparities.[2]

The main copper and gold deposits lie south of a line from the Firth of Lorne to the mouth of the Tay, particularly in south-west Scotland. Copper and bronze objects of the earliest phase of the British Bronze Age, and of types discussed below, are sporadic north of the Great Glen, have their most marked concentration in north-east Scotland along the Moray Firth; there is a fair scatter southwards from here along the coastal plain to the Firth of Forth and the eastern Border counties, and again in Galloway. The Nairn-Moray-Banff concentration is very remarkable: north of a line drawn from Inverness to Aberdeen there are not only some forty-five single finds and five hoards of axe-blades, of which those analysed have proved to be bronze, but nine stone open moulds for casting axe-blades, rings, and ingots.[3] Such a concentration of moulds is unique in the British Isles, rivalled only by the five found in north-east Ireland, and the only known local copper source to which the Moray Firth evidence of metallurgy could be related is that at Bona on Loch Ness. It seems inevitable that copper and ores or ingots must have been imported into the region from a distance, presumably along the Great Glen route. The further point in connexion with this north-east Scottish concentration is that it does not coincide with that of Beakers, the main weight of which

[1] cf. *Proc. Prehist. Soc.*, XXIII (1957), 91; Junghans *et al.*, *Metallanalysen kupferzeitliche und frühbronzezeitlicher Bodenfunde* (1960); Sangmeister in *Zephyrus*, XI (1960), 131.

[2] Distribution-map of metal sources in *Proc. Prehist. Soc.*, XVII (1951), 70.

[3] I am indebted here and elsewhere to Dr. Margaret Crichton Stewart for putting unpublished information at my disposal.

lies south-east of the area in question, particularly in the valleys of the Don and the Dee. And in general, the distribution of Beakers in Scotland is complementary to, rather than coincident with, the natural sources of copper and gold. In considering the source of tin it must be remembered that the coasting journey from the Moray Firth to the mouth of the Rhine —some 500 miles—is less than that down the Great Glen, and by the western sea routes to Cornwall, so continental sources cannot be ruled out.

Furthermore, when one tries to correlate the earliest metal industry of north Britain with the burials accompanied by Beakers or Food Vessels, one finds singularly little evidence of direct connexion. In two instances (Linlathen, Angus, and Glenforsa, Mull) Short-Necked Beakers were associated with copper or bronze knife-daggers; in one instance (Crawfurd, Lanarkshire), another such Beaker was found with a copper or bronze arm-ring;[1] two similar rings were found with a Food-Vessel burial at Kineff, Kincardineshire, and a single ring in a similar context at Ratho, West Lothian.[2] With two Food-Vessel burials (Balcalk, Forfarshire, and Kilmory, Argyll) were small copper or bronze awls: the former grave also contained a space-plate jet necklace, and with another such necklace at Melfort, Argyll, was found a pair of cuff-armlets almost certainly of bronze and not copper.[3] All that this evidence suggests is that metal objects were made or acquired by the users of both Beakers or Food Vessels indifferently, and infrequently buried with the dead. The hoard of bronze axes from Colleonard, Banffshire,[4] was contained in a pot with affinities to those usually classed as Cinerary Urns, and is again mentioned below.

Flat or slightly hammer-flanged axe-blades of copper or (as analyses are showing) more often bronze are the commonest type in the Scottish Early Bronze Age series, being known from fifteen hoards and about 160 single finds. Sub-types are perceptible, a distinction between the broad-butted form (common in Ireland)[5] and the narrow-butted version which probably reflects central European forms being fairly clear as elsewhere in the British Isles. In three hoards and in twelve stray finds we have

[1] Refs. in footnote 1, p. 81.

[2] Kineff, *Invent. Arch.*, GB 34; Ratho, Childe, *Scotland Before the Scots*, 107–18, no. 237.

[3] Childe, *op. cit.* nos. 74, 148; *Proc. Prehist. Soc.*, XIX (1953), 169; *Invent. Arch.*, GB 25.

[4] *Invent. Arch.*, GB 29.

[5] *Proc. Prehist. Soc.*, XXIII (1957), 102 and map fig. 5.

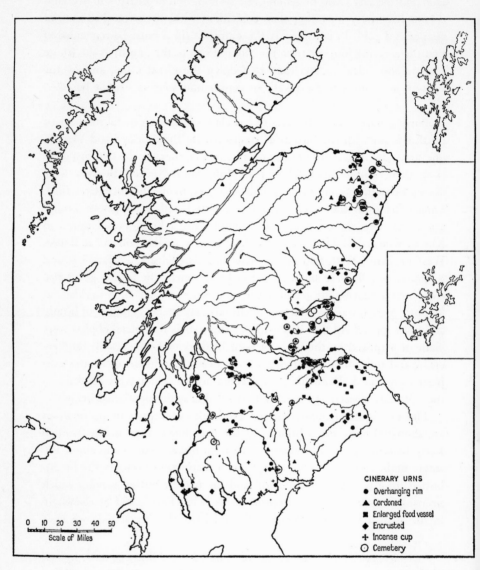

CINERARY URNS

● Overhanging rim
▲ Cordoned
■ Enlarged food vessel
◆ Encrusted
+ Incense cup
○ Cemetery

0 10 20 30 40 50
Scale of Miles

Fig. 13. Distribution of Cinerary Urns in Scotland (By Mr. J. Barber).

examples of the decorated axes of Megaw and Hardy's Types I and II, basically of Irish types.[1]

The English evidence shows that, as on the Continent, the Bell-Beaker people in these islands used the broad-tanged knife-dagger of copper. Three are known from Scotland, all strays, but two located in the area of heavy Beaker concentration in Aberdeenshire. A variant with tang and rivet (as at Glenforsa, Mull) seems characteristic of Short-Necked Beakers. The flat riveted daggers, found in a few instances associated with Long-Necked Beakers in England, but more often with stone battle-axes or with otherwise unaccompanied burials, are well represented in Scotland, and in one instance at least associated with Beaker burials. Some sixteen finds are recorded and (as elsewhere in the British Isles) two sub-types can be distinguished, one with the hilt-plates being cut at their lower edges to an omega-shaped outline, and the other with a broad W-shaped termination.[2] The former follows the normal Continental tradition, especially characteristic of central and northern Europe, and the latter may be an insular development. Analyses are showing such riveted daggers to be usually of bronze, in contradistinction to the copper tanged daggers of the earlier Bell-Beaker phase.

Two of the Scottish flat riveted daggers had their pommels decorated with ribbed gold bands (Skateraw, Dunbar, and Collessie, Fife) and similar bands have been found, once with a triple-ribbed dagger at Blackwaterfoot, Arran, and once with a Food Vessel (but without record of a dagger-blade) at Monikie, Perthshire.[3] Such enrichment of dagger-hafts is a characteristic of the Wessex Culture, and a precisely similar ribbed band was found with a grooved dagger-blade of the first phase of the culture in the Topped Mountain burial in Co. Fermanagh,[4] suggesting that there is an overlap of the flat riveted dagger with the flat grooved forms of the first phase of the Wessex Culture.[5]

To the earliest phase of the Bronze Age in Scotland, however, should belong the gold discs in the Broughty Ferry burial, and the remarkable

---

[1] *ibid.*, IV (1938), 272–307.

[2] *Proc. Soc. Ant. Scot.*, LXXXVIII (1954–56), 9.

[3] Skateraw, *Proc. Soc. Ant. Scot.*, XXVII (1892–93), 7; Collessie, *ibid.*, XII (1876–78), 439; Blackwaterfoot, *ibid.*, XXXVI (1901–02), 120; Monikie, *ibid.*, II (1854–57), 447.

[4] Coffey, *Bronze Age in Ireland* (1913), 56; Armstrong, *Cat. Gold Ornaments . . .* (1933), pl. X, no. 60.

[5] cf. my comments in *Culture and Environment: Essays in Honour of Sir Cyril Fox.*

gold basket-shaped ear-ornament from Orton in Morayshire. This, with its smaller bronze counterparts in the Migdale hoard, represents a type found twice associated with Bell-Beakers in Britain and known in Early Bronze Age contexts in northern Europe.[1] The well-known gold lunulae, as we shall see, should belong to a later phase of our Bronze Age.

At least two cists containing Beaker burials, and one with a Food Vessel, had cover-stones decorated with pecked or incised designs including concentric rings, spirals, and geometric patterns. These Scottish finds give the general context of a large number of similarly decorated stones, largely natural rock surfaces, in northern England and southern Scotland. The patterns themselves relate both the decorative art of the Boyne Culture passage graves and to other cup-and-ring carvings in Ireland, and the Crinan group with geometric patterns and representations of axes may show central European influences. The spirals, in Ireland as in Scotland, are hardly likely to be earlier than similar stone-carving in Malta and on the shaft-grave stelae at Mycenae, of the sixteenth century B.C. Close parallels to the cup-and-ring carvings of the British Isles exist in northern Spain, and it has been suggested that their presence in the metalliferous regions of south-western Ireland may be related to the activities of Galician miners and metal-workers.[2]

To this same general chronological horizon we must assign the settlement sites in Shetland, involving stone-built houses and field systems, and the so-called 'temple' of Stanydale. The houses have a basically oval plan with the entrance at one end, very thick walls, and inner post-settings to support the roof: the Stanydale site is an aggrandized version of the normal house, but its function is wholly inferential. In many places the houses are associated with field-clearance stone-heaps and ruined stone walls delimiting irregular areas which may indicate contemporary fields or garden plots. Querns and a deposit of burnt barley show that cereals were cultivated by the makers of the houses, whose material culture shows no evidence of a knowledge of metals, though an abundance of enigmatic rough stone implements occur on all sites, including pointed stone bars which may be elements of ploughs. The pottery is *sui generis*, though with reminiscences of Beaker and Neolithic styles, including the late Beacharra wares of the Hebrides, and some aspects of Rinyo-Clacton motifs.

[1] Orton, *Prehist. Scot.*, 102; Migdale, *Invent. Arch.*, GB 26; cf. *Palaeohist.*, V (1956), 53–71.

[2] *Journ. Roy. Soc. Ant. Ireland*, LXXVI (1946), 59–80.

Miniature stone battle-axes with slightly hollowed upper and lower faces, and a whetstone of a type associated with Long-Necked Beakers, give an approximate chronological position to this culture (which in some way should be ancestral to the earlier settlements at Jarlshof),[1] somewhere contemporary with the first phase of the Wessex Culture.

The foreign contacts of the Wessex Culture, not least those with the Mediterranean world, enable us to fix with relative precision a date in our British Bronze Age centred on the sixteenth century B.C. To review events in Scotland during the preceding four or five hundred years, we have seen that this was initially a period of immigration and colonization from the Low Countries and the Rhineland, predominantly affecting the east coast from the Moray Firth to the Border. The new settlers are distinguished by their burial rites from the earlier collective tomb tradition of the west and north, and the single-grave burial, often in a cist and infrequently under a mound, becomes the dominant form, used by people making Beakers, or Food Vessels, and probably by other groups whose customs did not include the burying of pots with their dead. Even if initially in a virtually stone-using economy, metallurgy in copper, gold, and later bronze, was soon developed by these people, probably in the main as the result of the arrival of technicians from central or northern European workshops, though the possibility of Iberian contacts as well cannot be wholly ruled out. Between this phase of entrance and consolidation, and the coming of the Celtic-speaking peoples discussed in Chapter IV, we can trace no certain further incomings of population to Scotland, though intensified trade and a resurgence of older traditions becomes apparent. To this second phase, the conventional Middle Bronze Age of archaeologists, we can now turn.

In terms of the Cairnpapple sequence (p. 86) we are now at the point when Phase III, the cairn with a Food-Vessel inhumation at its centre, is about to be enlarged to form the monument of Cairnpapple IV, with two cremation burials in its enlarged mound. But already in Cairnpapple I we have cremations, associated with ritual pits of Secondary Neolithic date, while eccentric to the central inhumation cist of Cairnpapple III was another, contemporary, cist containing an unaccompanied cremation. Furthermore, there are in Scotland a few Beaker burials with cremation instead of inhumation, and as we saw, a quarter of the Scottish Food-Vessel burials are by cremation. In fact, we have evidence in Scotland, as

[1] *Proc. Soc. Ant. Scot.*, LXXXIX (1955–56), 340.

elsewhere in the British Isles, that cremation and inhumation rites existed side-by-side in Neolithic Cultures at the beginning of the second millennium B.C.; that single-grave inhumation was a novel rite introduced from the Continent by Beaker and allied immigrants, and that by around the middle of the millennium the cremation rite began to reassert itself until it became completely dominant. The change-over was the result of a wholly indigenous process of assimilation, with a subsequent re-emergence of older traditions, analogous to the formation of the Secondary Neolithic cultures already described in Chapter I.

Cremation burials could be, and often were, made in a simple hole in the ground, in Scotland exceptionally under a mound, since something approaching an isotaph separating north and south Britain in terms of large-barrow burial or its virtual absence appears to persist into the period of universal cremation, though we must remember the potential destruction by ploughing of small low mounds. But containers for the burnt bones were also used: Food Vessels, for instance, and still more regularly, the large pottery vessels known as Cinerary Urns, again in the north usually without a covering mound or cairn, and often grouped in cemeteries.

These cremation cemeteries have been the subject of much misunderstanding, as have the pottery variants within the Cinerary-Urn class. The belief in a monogenetic origin, with subsequent developments spreading northwards from a hypothetical southern English centre, seems to have been held by Abercromby in respect of Cinerary Urns no less than of Beakers, with the result that types common in or restricted to the Highland Zone and Ireland, such as the Encrusted and especially the Cordoned Urns, had to be relegated to the status of late and degenerative derivatives from south English types such as the Collared or Overhanging Rim forms. The frequent grouping of cremation burials into cemeteries in Scotland, northern England, and Ireland, and sporadically elsewhere, was related in the first place to the Deverel-Rimbury 'urnfields' of Wessex (at that time assigned to the Late Bronze Age), and at longer remove to the Continental Urnfield Cultures at large: Fox indeed cited the northern Cremation cemeteries as a good example of his contention that the Highland Zone absorbed ideas originally introduced into Lowland Britain. As a result, it became generally accepted that no cremation cemetery in the British Isles could be earlier than the first Deverel-Rimbury 'urnfield', and that the urns and any grave-goods should as a result also fall into the

Late Bronze Age, and not too early within the phase, with an absolute date in the eighth century B.C.

The Law Park (St. Andrews) cremation cemetery with its encrusted and cordoned urns was in one study dated by the bronze two-edged razors which occurred with burials there to what was then conceived of as the Late Bronze Age, contemporary with leaf-shaped swords, socketed axes, and the South Lodge enclosure of the Deverel-Rimbury culture.[1] By a circular argument, in a subsequent study of two-edged razors in the British Bronze Age, the Law Park association was used in support of a Late Bronze Age date for the Class I razors under discussion, on the grounds that the urns were not far removed in time from that of the Deverel-Rimbury Culture—a date originally proposed on the grounds of the razors themselves![2] A recent reassessment of these Class I razors has, however, shown that their antecedents on the Continent belong to the Montelius II phase of the Northern Bronze Age, and that in Britain they mainly date from the second phase of the Wessex Culture and the period immediately following this, though occasional longer survival occurred.[3] Incidentally, the Deverel-Rimbury culture itself has now been placed in a Middle Bronze Age II phase, dated between c. 1200–1000 B.C.

With the recognition of Secondary Neolithic cremation cemeteries, however, there is no need to seek for an origin in a Highland Zone absorption of Deverel-Rimbury or other southern English burial rites for the Northern Bronze Age cemeteries under discussion. Over forty such sites are known in Scotland, and the burials in them constitute a good two-thirds of the total of all Cinerary-Urn burials north of the Border. The average number of burials is ten, the highest recorded is thirty-one, of which nineteen were not contained in urns—this occurrence of two types of burial is found in other sites. At least five cemeteries were within some form of a circular ritual enclosure: a Henge Monument at Broomend of Crichie, and a version of a similar monument at Loanhead of Daviot; a stone circle at Nith Lodge.[4] Such encircled flat cemeteries again occur in north England (e.g. in the Pennines), and must contain, not only the Henge Monument tradition, but that represented by the Pond Barrows of the Wessex Culture. Some cremation cemeteries are in mounds or cairns

[1] *Ant. Journ.*, VII (1927), 124.

[2] *Proc. Prehist. Soc.*, XII (1946), 124.

[3] *Univ. Lond. Inst. Arch. Ann. Reports*, XII (1956), 20.

[4] Broomend of Crichie, *Proc. Soc. Ant. Scot.*, LIV (1919–20), 154; Loanhead of Daviot, *ibid.*, LXX (1935–36), 278; Nith Lodg, *ibid.*, LXXII (1937–38), 235.

(as at New Cummock or Ardeer in Ayrshire) in a manner comparable to the well-known cairn of Knockast, Co. Westmeath, or those in north Yorkshire and Derbyshire.[1]

These cemeteries in themselves, then, show direct affinities with Secondary Neolithic ceremonial and burial customs, and the pottery, in fact, tells the same tale. It has been pointed out more than once that the techniques and motifs of ornament on the Encrusted Urns show strong affinities with those of the Rinyo-Clacton wares of the Late Neolithic phase, and there seems no reason for not accepting this comparison as valid, and regarding the urns as continuing this tradition into the Bronze Age. The Cordoned Urns, believed by Abercromby to be the degenerate end-products of the devolution of the Overhanging Rim type in regions north and west of its area of origin, are, however, susceptible of another and surely more convincing explanation. The strong resemblance, amounting in some cases to identity, between the Class II Ware in the Lough Gur Neolithic series, and the main types of Cordoned Urn, is too striking to be accidental, and the coarse undecorated flat based vessels from Rinyo tell the same tale.[2] There seems to be no valid reason for not regarding the Cordoned Urns as again derivative from Secondary Neolithic wares and perhaps of Irish origin, and the features they sometimes share in common with certain Overhanging Rim Urns as the result of these vessels also deriving from Secondary Neolithic pottery styles in regions farther south. The Colleonard hoard of decorated flat bronze axes mentioned above (p. 89) was contained in a pot which would, in the Abercromby classification, be regarded as a degenerate form approximating to a Cordoned Urn of the Late Bronze Age.

The cremation graves of the Scottish Bronze Age, whether isolated, grouped in cemeteries, within a ritual enclosure, or under a cairn, represent the re-emergence of a group of Secondary Neolithic ceremonial traditions after the initial impact of the single-grave inhumation rite, introduced from over the North Sea, had waned. There is no reason why some of these cremation burials may not be as early as the inhumations with Beakers or Food Vessels—certainly the widespread adoption of the cremation rite took place while the latter class of vessel was in funeral use.

[1] New Cumnock, *Proc. Soc. Ant. Scot., loc. cit.*; Ardeer, *ibid.*, XL (1905–06), 378; Knockast, *Proc. Royal Irish Acad.*, XLI (C) (L934), 232.
[2] *Proc. Roy. Arish. Acad.*, LVI (C) (1954), 333–9; Pls. xxxiii–xxxv; *Proc. Soc. Ant. Scot.*, LXXIII (1938–39), 24.

At the other end of the story, the tradition of such cremation burial presumably continued into and beyond the first arrival of new, Celtic, colonists, in the first millennium B.C. Can we find any fixed points within this long time-span?

It now seems clear that Abercromby's typological degeneration series of Cinerary Urns resulted from his arranging in a single assumed sequence several regional variants of pottery derived from Secondary Neolithic wares, his 'early' Cinerary Urns being a southern English development, and the 'late' Encrusted and Cordoned being characteristic of the Highland Zone and Ireland. We cannot use the pottery as a chronological guide, but must date the urns by means of other objects which may be associated with them. If no such association exists, the vessel in question must remain undated except within the broad limits indicated above. The problem is further complicated by the fact that during the Middle Bronze Age in Britain the wholesale adoption of the cremation burial was accompanied by a decline in the custom of depositing grave-goods with the dead. On the other hand, the middle of the second millennium B.C. was a period of active trade throughout Europe, and in the British Isles, and so far as Scotland is concerned we must remember that while self-sufficient in copper, tin could only be obtained from the south-western corner of England or from the European continent. The development of a fully bronze-using economy in the British Isles seems to date from the first phase of the Wessex Culture, and seems to indicate the first decisive establishment of trade relations with Cornish tin-streamers. Tin was an economic necessity, but the trade routes once in active use, objects other than the metal could be brought for barter and exchange from south to north.

The rise of the Wessex Culture in southern England, as is well known, can be given some chronological precision on account of the equations that can be established not only with the Central European Bronze Age sequence, but with the Mediterranean world and ultimately that of Mycenean Greece. A date centred on 1550 B.C. for the first phase of the culture is reasonably certain: a phase in which *inter alia* inhumation burial is predominant, and the daggers in men's graves are of the flat triangular, grooved type. In the second phase of the culture, cremation supersedes inhumation as the burial rite, and the warriors' daggers are of the ogival type with thickened midrib.[1] It is in this phase that the main period of

[1] *Univ. Lond. Inst. Arch. Ann. Reports*, X (1954), 37.

importation of faience beads seems to occur, with a likely date in the fifteenth or fourteenth century B.C.[1]

In both phases the exotic objects in the Wessex Culture can be divided into two groups—those which derive from or reflect the fashions of central Europe, and those which are imports or copies of imports from the Mediterranean. In its first phase the culture seems virtually confined to southern England: Wessex itself, with extensions along the Channel Coast (especially westwards to Cornwall), and in East Anglia. It seems likely that most inhumation burials accompanied by flat riveted bronze daggers, including the Scottish examples with gold-mounted hilts already mentioned, should have a chronological position contemporary with this phase, and probably also other dagger types with midribs (such that with a burial at the Wester Mains of Auchterhouse)[2] and also the extended burials in massive cists noted by Childe.[3]

In the second phase we find characteristic cremation burials and stray finds of metal objects extending into Derbyshire and Yorkshire, and up the Irish Sea to Scotland. The types which we can use as characteristic include the ogival daggers and their congeners already mentioned; spearheads of Arreton Down type; narrow-butt cast-flange axes of central European derivation; bone copies of ring-head or crutch-head bronze pins with the same origin; faience beads and other ornaments; and stone battle-axes of Snowshill and derivative types. To these should be added, in all probability, contemporary Highland Zone developments such as the copper or bronze halberds and the space-plate necklaces of jet or lignite. The single amber space-plate necklace from Scotland mentioned below must certainly be a Wessex Culture export.

We may therefore use the occurrence of objects such as those just listed, all products or derivatives of the Wessex Culture between c. 1550 and c. 1350, to give us a date for cremation burials outside the Wessex area in which they are included as grave-goods. To return to the cremation cemeteries already discussed, of the hundred or so known in the British Isles about one-quarter contain one or more burials with such Wessex Culture objects, implying their use during this phase. In Scotland we may notice, for instance, the stone battle-axes buried as weapons of prestige at Stranraer,[4] Nith Lodge, or Broomend of Crichie; the ivory belt-hook at

[1] Proc. Prehist. Soc., XXII (1956), 37–84.
[2] Proc. Soc. Ant. Scot., XXXII (1897–98), 211.
[3] Scotland Before the Scots, 119.   [4] Proc. Soc. Ant. Scot., LXXVI (1941–42), 79.

Brackmont Mill;[1] faience beads from many burials; the bone ring-head pin from Cairnpapple IV and a crutch-head from Balniel;[2] some at least of the Class I razors, and the accessory vessels or 'incense cups', which again seem to have Wessex Culture affiliations, from many burials.

Even more exotic objects can be detected. The cremation cemetery in a barrow at Gilchorn in Angus produced, in one burial, a glass bead of Eighteenth Dynasty Egyptian type [1580–1344 B.C.—a closer dating is given by another such bead from Mycenae in a Late Helladic II (fifteenth-century) context].[3] And with another burial in the same cemetery was a small bronze blade, unifacially ribbed and with notched base, paralleled in the British Isles only in another cremation cemetery, secondary to a chambered tomb, at Harristown, Co. Waterford, where it was associated with a ring-head bone pin and a faience quoit-bead, in a Cinerary Urn. Another burial was contained in an urn which bears a striking and detailed resemblance to that from Cairnpapple IV, which contained the ring-head pin. The bronze blades of Gilchorn-Harristown type are known elsewhere only in Iberia and the south of France.[4]

Such features as these, and the distribution of finds of the types mentioned above, strongly suggest that it was traffic along the western seaways connected with the tin trade that brought these novel or exotic objects to Scotland, by a route by way of St. George's Channel and the Irish Sea to landfalls in the Luce Bay region and along the Ayrshire coast. Whether we are dealing solely with trade exchanges or with some small degree of settlement by traders is uncertain.

We have still to discuss one of the most interesting pieces of evidence of contacts between the Wessex Culture and Scotland, that provided by the space-plate necklaces already referred to more than once, and in north Britain frequently associated with Food Vessels in burials. The necklace type represented is one in which multiple strings of beads are spaced and held separate by flat oblong 'spacers' transversely perforated; in order to produce a crescent-shaped arrangement of the beads the space-plates, by means of Y-shaped or similar perforations, can be made to increase the number of strings symmetrically, though not all space-plate necklaces are so constructed.

[1] ibid., LXXV (1940–41), 205.   [2] ibid., L (1915–16), 302.

[3] Proc. Prehist. Soc., XXII (1956), 59.

[4] Harristown, Journ. Roy. Soc. Ant. Ireland, LXXI (1941), 139; Proc. Prehist. Soc., loc. cit. (faience bead); for notched blades, Childe in Arch. Prehist. Levantina, IV (1953), 16; Sandars, Bronze Age Cultures in France (1957), 31.

Such necklaces made of amber are known in the Wessex Culture, and, more than that, in the Mycenae shaft graves and at least one other Mycenaean tomb: they (or versions of them) again occur in south-west Germany and eastern France in graves of the Reinecke Bronze Age B phase.[1] The chronological complications involved in these occurrences need not detain us here, for within Britain it is clear that the amber necklaces fit into an earlier archaeological context than do those of jet, whatever the absolute dating. Furthermore, it is in the amber space-plates alone that we have the phenomenon of 'complex' borings (as in the Mycenae Grave-Circle B, Kakovatos, and some south German spacers), while in the jet necklaces there are simple Y-borings, or even cruder elbow-boring at the edges of the plates, though the ornament on the plates not infrequently suggests a skeuomorph of the complex boring of the amber prototypes. In Scotland we have one example of an amber necklace with complex borings, that from a cremation burial in one of the Knowes of Trotty in Orkney, and here it seems that the space-plates were broken and re-used before their deposition with the burial.[2]

But the popularity of the necklace type is attested by the numerous jet or lignite versions (over thirty-five are known from Scotland), and as was pointed out in the original study of the type, the well-known gold lunulae, common in Ireland and represented by four examples in Scotland, must be a copy of a space-plate necklace of some kind.[3] The fact that the engraved ornament of the lunulae not only copies in its oblong panels the arrangement of the space-plates of the prototype, but that within these panels a skeuomorph of the pattern formed by complex borings is often present, implies that the lunulae and the jet necklaces are both derivative from amber originals. There is no evidence from associated finds to date the lunulae, but in Scotland jet necklaces occur twice in contexts which can be approximately dated. At Melfort in Argyll such a necklace was associated with a pair of cuff-shaped bronze armlets decorated with lenticular bosses comparable to those on the great gold ornament from Mold and its Continental counterparts such as the Schifferstadt and Etzeldorf objects, referable to Montelius II B/C and Reinecke B, with a date of c. 1350–1250 B.C. on current chronologies, and in Britain representing a

---

[1] *Germania*, XXIV (1940), 99; *ibid.* XXXIII (1955), 316; Hachmann, *Frühe Bronzezeit im West. Ostseebegiet* . . . (1957), 176–8; Sandars, *op. cit.*, 72–77, and in *Antiquity*, XXXIII (1959), 292.

[2] *Invent. Arch.*, GB 33.

[3] *Proc. Soc. Ant. Scot.*, L (1915–16), 201; *ibid.*, LXIII (1928–29), 186.

phase immediately after that of the Wessex Culture. At Kilmartin, also in Argyll, another necklace was found with a bowl-type Food Vessel which may be equated with northern European gold bowls of Montelius III, and therefore somewhat later than Melfort. The two finds are consistent in implying that the jet necklaces are likely as a group to be derivative from, and chronologically later than, the amber versions of the Wessex Culture.[1]

Another type referable to a context overlapping with the Wessex Culture is the copper or bronze halberd, of which a couple of dozen examples have been found in Scotland. The presence in the Wessex Culture of three miniature halberd-pendants confirms the chronological position for halberds implied by Continental finds in Reinecke A1/A2. The halberd has usually been considered an Irish invention, but the case for a central European origin is now being put forward, and has much to be said for it: it should be noted that the so-called 'ring-rivets' which are characteristically central and northern European, occur on at least two Irish specimens.[2] By some curious conservatism, halberds seem to have been made of copper as a deliberate choice, even though true bronze was by then in general use.

In the period following these Wessex Culture contacts, it becomes more and more difficult to correlate the cremation burials, now usually without associated grave-goods save for the urn containing the bones, with the metal types. An Encrusted Urn and an unlooped palstave of early type seem, however, to have been associated in a Roxburghshire find,[3] and some of the Class I razors must belong to this later Middle Bronze Age phase. In it, too, would come the typologically early socketed spears with angular base to the blade and loops on the socket, as well as the leaf-shaped types with loops at the base of the blade which occur on the Continent as exports in contexts ranging from Montelius II (Liesbüttel) to Reinecke D (Wiesloch): the general date suggested by such association would be around the middle of the thirteenth century B.C. To the same general chronological position in our Middle Bronze Age can be assigned the rapiers, elongated versions of the earlier ogival dagger, often with trapeze-shaped butts in the manner of contemporary north European

[1] *Proc. Prehist. Soc.*, XIX (1953), 169–72.
[2] Irish examples include O'Riordain's no. 109 ('Ireland') and Breaghwy (*Arch.* LXXXVI (1937), 305; *Proc. Prehist. Soc.*, XII (1946) 155.
[3] *Trans. Glasgow Arch. Soc.*, NS XIV (1956), 31.

developments. There is a remarkable hoard of six rapiers said to have been found in the ditch of a circular earthwork at Drumcoltran in Kirkcudbrightshire, and another is included in a hoard from Glen Trool in the same county.[1] This hoard also includes a twisted bronze torc similar to others in Somerset finds, within Hawkes's Middle Bronze II, c. 1200–1000 B.C. In the same hoard was a blue glass bead very similar to one from Knackyboy Cairn, Isles of Scilly, where it was probably rather later than a worn star-shaped faience bead: the Knackyboy glass beads have good parallels in the Prosymna Mycenaean series ranging through Late Helladic times until c. 1200 B.C.[2] Glentrool, then, would date to the final phase of our Middle Bronze Age, c. 1200–1000 B.C.

The next phase in Scottish prehistory was to be the intensified central and northern Europe contacts which were to culminate in the arrival of the first certainly Celtic-speaking peoples in Britain. Of the linguistic affiliations of the earlier peoples with whom we have been concerned in this chapter we have no certain knowledge, but there is some agreement among philologists that there is at least a possibility that certain components in the make-up of the British Beaker immigrations may represent peoples who spoke Indo-European, though not Celtic, dialects. If the correlations which have recently been suggested between Indo-European languages and certain forms of social structure and organization be accepted, the 'heroic' society which the thesis demands might be reflected in the richly-furnished graves suggestive of a warrior-aristocracy which exist sporadically in the Beaker Cultures and much more markedly in the Wessex Culture.

The picture of the cultural components of Early and Middle Bronze Scotland here presented differs in many respects from those previously constructed. The clear-cut, tidy divisions between 'Neolithic' and 'Bronze Age' Beakers, Food Vessels, and Cinerary Urns hardly stand up to scrutiny. We must visualize a state of affairs in which, while Secondary Neolithic communities such as Skara Brae were still flourishing in the Orkneys, and chambered tombs still being built and used in the west and north of Scotland, new colonists arriving on the east coast, established themselves, and before long were not only using but manufacturing copper and bronze

[1] Drumcoltran, Roy. Comm. Anc. Mons. (Scot.), *Kirkcudbright Invent.* (1914), no. 280; Glen Trool, *Proc. Soc. Ant. Scot.*, LV (1920–21), 29.

[2] Stone in *Ant. Journ.*, XXXII (1952), 30, and in *Proc. Roy. Irish Acad.*, LVI (C) (1954), 357, no. 63. *cf. Proc. Prehist. Soc.*, XXV (1959), 144.

tools and weapons and gold ornaments. The burial rite of these people was that of individual inhumation often accompanied by a pottery Beaker; the rite was shared by other communities, some placing a pot of Food-Vessel type in the grave, others no pottery at all. The cremation rite, the encircled cemeteries, and the vessels of Encrusted and Cordoned Urn type, have Secondary Neolithic antecedents, and graves with such pottery may well overlap in time the inhumation burials with Food Vessels or even with Beakers. Conversely, the Food Vessels, and the jet space-plate necklaces often associated with them, must continue in use beyond the period of the later Wessex Culture, to which many Scottish cremation burials in Cinerary Urns belong. It is a picture of greater complexity than the old neatly arranged sequence of Beakers, Food Vessels, and Cinerary Urns in various stages of assumed degeneration, but one which seems more likely to approximate to the long past events which produced the archaeological evidence we now study.

Note on the Maps

The general distribution-patterns for the period under review in this chapter have been shown on four maps, all compiled by my pupils in the Department of Prehistoric Archaeology in the University of Edinburgh, and reproduced here by their kind permission. I have to thank Miss Rosemary Crawford for the Beaker maps, figs. 10 and 11, Mr. Derek Simpson for that of Food-Vessel pottery, fig. 12, and Mr. James Barber for that of Cinerary Urns and allied pottery, fig. 13.

CHAPTER FOUR

The Coming of the Celts

Aɴʏ discussion of the coming of the Celts to Scotland must rest on an appraisal of the use of the words 'Celt' and 'Celtic', and from that standpoint progress may then be possible towards some correlation between philological and historical pointers, together with the archaeological interpretation of distinctive traits in ancient material cultures.

It was the initial research of a Scots scholar, George Buchanan (1506–82), that led to the adoption of the term Celtic for that group of languages chief amongst which are Irish, Scots Gaelic, Welsh, and Breton. He it was who first demonstrated their parentage in the language of the Celts, a people well known to Greek and Latin writers of antiquity. It must be made clear from the outset, however, that the name Κελτοι (*Celtae*) was used by Classical writers only in relation to Continental peoples, and that there is no existing evidence to show that it was used by native, or foreigner, for the inhabitants of Britain or Ireland. In speaking of Celtic as a philological classification, the definition is no older than Buchanan's use, coming only into general acceptance after the publication, in 1707, of Edward Lluyd's first volume of *Archaeologia Britannica*. To the Greeks and Romans there were indeed Celts, but their language was no more than another barbarian tongue merely to be ignored as a phenomenon in itself. This point is important, for it follows that in the ancient world the Celts were definable ethnologically. They were a barbarian people of trans-Alpine Europe recognizable by their total national characteristics in appearance, arms, manners, and customs, in the same way as were distinguished other peoples such as the Scythians, Persians, or Ethiopians.[1]

The use of the term Celtic in a philological sense is, of course, justifiable provided that it is recognized to rest on an ultimate ethnological distinction. The distribution of Celtic place-names in Continental Europe, and the native names and words recorded in the Classics as directly related to the Celts, demonstrate this proposition, but a distinction must be observed between the Celts as a major people in middle and western Europe to the days of Julius Caesar and those Celtic-speaking insular peoples who emerged in post-Roman times under local names, and without recognition even of their partial ancestry in the Continental Celts. Whatever degree of fusion may have taken place between indigenous populations and the prehistoric Celtic intruders to these islands, there is, of course, no question but that a predominately Celtic speech, and way of life, continued in many parts after the withdrawal of Roman power, but it must be incorrect to speak of other than the Irish, the Scots, or the Welsh, in medieval and modern times. The Celts had long disappeared as an ethnological and political reality in those parts of Europe for which they had been historically vouched.

In order to understand the premises on which archaeological evidence for Celtic settlement in Scotland can be based it will be necessary to state briefly the chronological and geographical range of the Celts in mainland Europe, and to review the material culture associations which should be sufficiently valid to postulate the presence of Celtic communities living beyond the orbit of contemporary history.

The earliest references to the Celts, by Hecataeus, and by Herodotus, show these people to have been known to the Greeks already by the late sixth and early fifth centuries B.C.[2] These are merely passing references which seem to imply that knowledge of the Celts was nothing new, but Herodotus' discussion of western Mediterranean, and Danubian, geography provides evidence for their widespread distribution in his own time.[3] In the far west they were located both beyond the Pillars of Hercules, as well as at the eastern end of the Pyrenees, and around the Gulf of Lions to behind Massilia. Although Herodotus was misled about the source of

[1] For a general discussion of the Celts, see T. G. E. Powell, *The Celts*, London, 1958.

[2] E. H. Warmington, *Greek Geography*, London, 1934, for the majority of early references.

[3] *Books*, II, 33, and IV, 49.

the Danube, believing it to flow from the Pyrenees, it may be that he had an independent report, deriving in fact from Danubian trade routes, that the river rose amongst the Celts. His acquaintance with affairs on the Lower Danube would reasonably suggest that he would have sought information on its origin in that quarter, and hearing of the Celts in this association as well, he could easily have deduced their geographical identity, and consequently the Pyrenean source of the river.

It is only at second hand, and in a much later composition, that Hecataeus' information is available.[1] He also knew of the Celts behind Massilia, but, in another fragment, he referred to a Celtic town named Nyrax, and this place is considered by some to have been the forerunner of Noreia, at the eastern end of the Alps. The pattern indicated by these ancient literary sources finds substance in archaeological evidence for the existence of an extensive zone in middle and western Europe, principally the result of migration and settlement, and, throughout, exhibiting common origins in material culture, burial rites, and fortifications. In archaeological terminology this is the Hallstatt iron-using culture which, with regional variations, had achieved its greatest expansion within the seventh century B.C.[2] This is the inescapable archaeological background of the Celts of Hecataeus and Herodotus, and it is important to realize that all this is antecedent to that optimum of Celtic barbaric prosperity witnessed in the La Tène Culture, and of the great expansion of the Celts in the late fifth and fourth centuries B.C.[3] In this later expansion the Celts overran Italy, and the Balkans, but did not pass south of the Pyrenees. In the Iberian Peninsula there had been a migration from the region of the Swiss Lakes and the Upper Rhine which followed the Rhône valley and the Gulf of Lions to the eastern end of the Pyrenees, but these were people mainly of the Late Urnfield Culture with some Hallstatt elements, and the migration is dated on present concepts to the early part of the seventh century B.C. The significance of place-names in the Peninsula that are philologically Celtic may thus be seen in a sharper light, and they provide a valuable chronological signpost for the development of Celtic as a European language, whereas Celtic placenames elsewhere in Europe cannot be

[1] F. Jacoby, *Fragmente der griechischen Historiker*, vol. 1, Berlin, 1923.

[2] V. G. Childe, *Prehistoric Migrations in Europe*, Oslo, 1950, 214–230; for a general account of the period.

[3] J. M. de Navarro, 'The Coming of the Celts', *Cambridge Ancient History*, vol. VII (1928) for the expansion of the La Tène Celts.

demonstrated as necessarily earlier than the expansion of the La Tène Celts.[1]

With these basic considerations on the Celts now set forth, attention must turn to the entirely prehistoric regions north of the Alps so as eventually to trace northward movements of these people in the direction of the British Isles.

The widespread group of interrelated cultures loosely classified as Hallstatt, that can in part be dated on the evidence of Greek and Etruscan associated finds to the sixth century B.C.,[2] represent but a stage in an archaeological sequence that had developed its principal characteristics at the beginning of the first millennium B.C. The formative area, for all that part of Europe concerned in the present study, was the Upper Danubian basin from the Bavarian Forest to the Black Forest, and from the high Alps to the Swabian and Franconian Jura. This region, together with Lower and Upper Austria, the Tyrol, and Central Bohemia, formed what has been called the North Alpine province of the Urnfield Cultures of middle Europe.[3] The economy was based on settled farming and an extensive bronze industry in weapons and tools. The characteristic burial rite was cremation in an urn with deposition in a large flat cemetery, although barrow burial was frequent from area to area.

From this primary North Alpine region there had taken place extensive movements into the Rhine valley,[4] to around the Swiss lakes,[5] and in one

---

[1] H. Rix, 'Zur Verbreitung und Chronologie einiger Keltischer Ortsnamen', *Goessler Festschrift* 99–107, (1954) for a study of certain Celtic place-name forms in Gaul and Spain. The Celtic river names in N.W. Germany, discussed by H. M. Chadwick *Ridgeway Essays* (1913), may date back to settlement of the region in Urnfield or Hallstatt times, but the subsequent expansion of the La Tène Celts is perhaps more relevant, as witnessed in the Teutonic *walh*—compounds which must be later than the Teutonic adaption of the Celtic tribal name Volcae as explained by H. M. Chadwick, *The Nationalities of Europe* (1945), 150 and 153.

[2] J. J. Hatt, 'Commerce grec du VIᵉ et commerce italo-grec du Vᵉsiècle', *Revue archéologique de l'Est et du Centre-Est*, VI (1955), 150–2 Dijon, for summary of this sixth and fifth centuries B.C. trade.

[3] V. G. Childe, *The Danube in Prehistory*, Oxford, 1929, 334–53. For recent detailed study see H. Müller-Karpe, *Beiträge zur Chronologie der Urnenfelderzeit nördlich und südlich der Alpen*, Berlin, 1959.

[4] W, Kimmig, *Die Urnenfelderkultur in Baden*, Berlin, 1940; K. Tackenberg, *Fundkarten zur Vorgeschichte der Rheinprovinz*, Bonn, 1954.

[5] E. Vogt, 'Die spätbronzezeitliche Keramik der Schweiz und ihre Chronologie', *Denkschriften der schweizerischen naturforschenden Gesellschaft*, LXVI (1930), Zurich. 'Der Beginn der Hallstattzeit in der Schweiz', *Jahrbuch der Schweizerischen Gesellschaft für Urgeschichte*, XL (1949/50), 209–31, Frauenfeld.

direction to the Rhône and thence to Languedoc and the Pyrenees.[1] The Middle Rhenish area of colonization became itself an important centre of dispersion, principally to the Moselle, and the head-waters of the Seine,[2] as well as to the Lower Rhine, and into southern Holland and Belgium.[3]

The original North Alpine Urnfield Cultures were the outcome of amalgamation between indigenous crafts and new impulses, the latter especially in improved husbandry, metal techniques, and other skills, all of more easterly origins. The degree to which an immigrant population from the Middle Danube played a leading part in these changes is disputable, but some intruders would seem necessary to explain the initial stimulus. It is certain, however, that in the Rhenish zone there was considerable immigration, but also degrees of fusion with the indigenous people varying from district to district. The construction of barrows for the lodgement of urn cemeteries, together with the continuance of native ceramic traditions, as in the case of the Lower Rhenish barrows and fret-stamped pottery, demonstrate the essentially mixed nature of the peripheral cultures.

What is important for an appreciation of the subsequent iron-using peoples of the North Alpine zone, and its extensions, is that there was essential continuity in all the basic elements of material culture and ecological pattern, from the establishment of the regional Urnfield groups right down to the fifth century, to the time of Herodotus, and to the birth of the La Tène Culture of the historical Celts about the time of his death.

The development of an iron-using economy, and the other changes which gave these varied cultures a 'Hallstatt complexion' seem to have been brought about by stimuli imposed by intrusive overlords who may have been quite few in number, and by the quickening in trade relations that they set in motion. However much these overlords may have brought together the Urnfield groups in a new political unity, the essential elements in language and institutions, contributory to the formation of the Celts, would seem to have existed already amongst the North Alpine peoples.

[1] W. Kimmig, 'Zur Urnenfelderkultur in Südwesteuropa,' *Goessler Festschrift*, 41–98, N. K. Sandars, *Bronze Age Cultures in France*, Cambridge 1957.

[2] W. Kimmig, 'Où en est l'étude de la civilisation des Champs d'Urnes en France.' *Revue Archéologique de l'Est et du Centre-Est*, III (1952), 137–72, and V (1954), 7–28, 209–32, Dijon.

[3] K. Tackenberg, *op cit.*, S. J. De Laet, J. A. E. Nenquin, P. Spitaels, *Contributions à l'étude de la civilisation des champs d'urnes en Flandre*, Brugge, 1958.

The considerations already stated for the Pyrenean region would seem to require this deduction.

The sequence of events which brought about the creation of true Hallstatt Cultures in the Rhenish zone, most relevant to Britain, can only be understood in the light of the prehistory of Bavaria, from whence the new factors immediately came.

In the final phase in Bavaria of the Late Bronze Age,[1] some cremation graves contain innovations that are not the result of local developments. The first is the presence of sheet bronze vessels and other objects of Upper Adriatic provenance,[2] and the second is that of bronze horse-gear, mainly snaffle bits with characteristic rings and cheek-pieces of close east European, even Oriental, affinities. The very complicated problem of the source of the horse-gear cannot be ventured upon here,[3] and it must suffice to say that in Bavaria it is certainly intrusive. Furthermore, that whatever problems exist in the typology and chronology of the horse-gear over its total distribution, Bavaria lies on the western edge of that distribution, and the intrusion of horsemen at this stage may have been little more than an occasional event. It does not appear that within Bavaria the Late Urnfield horse-gear led directly to the development of the types that are present as a major feature in the ensuing graves of the first iron-using Hallstatt Culture of the same area.[4]

In addition to horse-gear, the other Hallstatt innovations were principally the long iron sword, and its bronze copy, the bronze winged chape for the scabbard, and, for personal adornment, pins of types with swan's neck and cup head. The pottery which is generally of high excellence shows both local Urnfield and exotic strains. The burial rite of the Hallstatt I horsemen was also a departure from North Alpine practice. In the finest tombs, the warrior's body was laid out unburnt on a four-

[1] Variously known as 'Hallstatt B' or 'Jüngere Urnenfelderkultur'. Here referred to as Late Urnfield, V. G. Childe (1948) suggested the term 'Bronze Period F', but this has not been generally adopted.

[2] These are the North Adriatic exports referred to by Hawkes, 'From Bronze to Iron Age: Middle Europe, Italy, and the North and West', *PPS*, XIV (1948), 196–218. As he shows, they are not exclusively of Italian manufacture (214–15).

[3] G. Kossack, 'Pferdegeschirr aus Gräbern der älteren Hallstattzeit Bayerns', *Jahrbuch des Römisch-Germanischen Zentralmuseums Mainz*, I (1953), 111–78, for types and distribution maps.

[4] The key area for the western ramifications of the iron-using Hallstatt Cultures is southern Bavaria, now studied in detail by G. Kossack, *Südbayern während der Hallstattzeit*, Röm-Germ. Forsch., XXIV (1959).

wheeled waggon, or on its dismantled parts. The grave was equipped with a full complement of weapons, pottery vessels and joints of meat for a feast. The bridles for two, sometimes three, horses were included, but horses, if slain, were not put in the tomb. The tomb itself normally consisted of a wood-built rectangular chamber, and it was surmounted by a large tumulus or barrow. This ritual would seem to combine possible steppeland and Etruscan elements; the horse gear and wooden chamber representing the former, while the hearse with extended inhumation suggests the latter. The ritual use of a vehicle was, of course, nothing new amongst the Urnfielders, as is shown by the burnt remains of a four-wheeled cart with a cremation grave from Hart a.d. Alz, Upper Bavaria,[1] and the wheeled cauldron with a cremation from Milaveč in Bohemia.[2]

These waggon graves are few in number as compared with Hallstatt I inhumation and cremation graves, under barrows, variously containing swords and horse-gear. These lesser graves represent the main spread of Hallstatt I warriors west and north, to Switzerland, and through Württemburg to the Rhine and beyond.

It should be noted, meanwhile, that the waggon graves in the Upper Elbe valley, in Bohemia, form an important centre for the diffusion northwards towards the Baltic of Hallstatt I metal types. These Bohemian tombs must be regarded as of close affinity in their contents with the Bavarian, and on this basis they must come within the Hallstatt Culture proper, following the unity of that region with the North Alpine Urnfield province. The waggon graves in Bohemia and Bavaria must be of the same date, if the former may not in part be slightly older.

For the sake of clarity a few words must be said at this point on the site of Hallstatt, and the application of its name to the cultures under discussion. Hallstatt is situated deep in the Salzkammergut, and its fame derives from the rich cemetery of the Iron Age population which was first excavated in the mid-nineteenth century. The subsequent recognition of similar grave goods elsewhere led to the widespread adoption of the name as a convenient descriptive label. The prosperity at Hallstatt rested on the extraction of salt, by mining and from saline springs, and this much-prized commodity commanded a high barter rate resulting in the

[1] H. Müller-Karpe (1955), 'Das urnenfelderzeitliche Wagengrab von Hart a.d. Alz, *Bayerische Vorgeschichtsblätter*, XXI (1955), 46–75.

[2] N. Åberg, *Chronologie*, Teil V: Mitteleuropäische Hochbronzezeit, Stockholm (1935), 51, fig. 88.

acquisition of luxury objects brought over long distances.[1] In particular the Hallstatt graves were rich in bronze vessels and brooches of Upper Adriatic provenance. Both periods of the iron-using Hallstatt Culture (I and II, or C and D) are represented in the type-site cemetery.[2] The long iron sword is present in the older graves, but there is no horse-gear, nor would this be expected in such a mountainous environment.

The material from Hallstatt is certainly to be classified with that from other sites in Upper Austria as well as in Bavaria and Bohemia, but the application of the name to the contemporary and perhaps older, Iron Age Cultures east and south of the Styrian Alps, as in the case of the so-called East Alpine and Bosnian 'Hallstatt' Cultures, is misleading. These latter with the Villanovan of north-eastern Italy, formed a zone around the Upper Adriatic in which advanced metal working flourished, stimulated by Etruscan and perhaps other East Mediterranean implantations, and founded on cultures of Middle Danubian, not North Alpine, growth.[3]

The chronological range of the first phase of the Hallstatt Culture (I, or C) in, and around, Bavaria is generally considered to have been from within the first half of the seventh century B.C., and lasting to the mid-sixth, when considerable changes in fashion, in weapons and ornaments, make necessary the distinction of a second phase, itself divisible into two. The changes in characteristic assemblages from one to the other period were due at first to continued trade-borne influences from the Upper Adriatic province. There is nothing in the North Alpine zone to suggest further inroads of settlers or overlords. The Hallstatt II (or D) graves are more numerous than those of the preceding phase, and the impression is that of a more widely shared culture, and a more settled state of affairs, with numerous petty chieftains equipped with an armoury

[1] R. Pittioni, *Urgeschichte des Österrichischen Raumes*, Vienna, 1954 for most recent discussion. The element *hall* in the place-name has been claimed as Illyrian, a language parallel to Celtic, but it is more probably older than the definitive emergence of either. For detailed study of the Hallstatt cemetery, see now K. Kromer, *Das Gräbfeld von Hallstatt*, Firenze, 1959.

[2] Hallstatt I and II, following Childe (1948), Periods C and D, if the alternative system is followed.

[3] H. Hencken, *Indo-European Languages and Archaeology*, American Anthropological Association, Memoir no. 84 (1955), 26–28, and references therein. This, of course, applies to the Terremare Urnfield Culture of the River Po, and not to the recently discovered urnfields south of the central Alpine passes in the Ticino, and province of Milano, reported by F. Rittatore in: 'Wissenschaftlicher Teil, III: Bronzezeit', *Jahrbuch der Schweizerischen Gesellschaft für Urgeschichte*, XLIV (1954–55), 63–68, Frauenfeld.

that has been suggested as having been more suitable for the pleasures of the chase than for warfare.

Some chieftains, perhaps the members of a paramount dynasty, or royal tribe, were given resplendent waggon burial, and a significant aspect of this matter is the removal of the geographical centre of these waggon tombs, by Hallstatt II times, from the old Bohemian-Bavarian region to Württemburg and the Rhine, with outliers in Switzerland and Burgundy.[1] It was for the benefit of these princes that was opened up the trade with Massilia by way of the Rhône, and with the Etruscans, also by that route, and then by direct central Alpine passes.[2] This constitutes an important final achievement of the Hallstatt Culture which then gave way in the mid-fifth century to its remarkable offspring, the La Tène Culture, first centred on the Middle Rhine, and characterized by two-wheeled war chariots in the princely tombs.[3]

The complexities of the disruption and migration of Urnfield communies consequent upon the appearance, in at least some areas, of the Hallstatt I warriors, and the developments in material culture resulting from the intermingling of these elements elsewhere cannot be traced here. It must suffice for the present purpose to draw attention to three areas from which emanated influences with direct bearing on the eastern littoral of Britain as a whole, and of particular relevance to the Celtic problem in Scotland.

In the West Alpine region of the Swiss lakes and in the Jura, the Urnfield population lived largely in crannog-type dwellings, and carried on a flourishing bronze industry.[4] The area was overrun by Hallstatt I warriors, and they are considered to have been largely responsible for the destruction and abandonment of many of the lake settlements, and for the departure of some of the local communities. The climatic deterioration associated with the term *Sub-Atlantic* was also doubtless contributory.[5] The displaced communities moved north, and some eventually found their way

---

[1] S. Schiek, 'Das Hallstattgrab von Vilsingen', *Goessler Festschrift*, (1954) 150–67. See especially map, p. 156. The distribution of Hallstatt D bronze cauldrons is also significant. *v.* C. F. C. Hawkes and M. A. Smith, 'On some buckets and cauldrons of the Bronze and Early Iron Ages', *Antiquaries Journal* xxxvii (1957) 131–198.

[2] T. G. E. Powell, *op. cit.* (1958), 94–99 and 113, for references to original studies.

[3] P. Jacobsthal, *Early Celtic Art*, Oxford, 1944.

[4] V. G. Childe, *The Danube in Prehistory*, Oxford, 1929, 354–8.

[5] G. Smolla (1954), 'Der "Klimasturz" um 800 vor Chr. und seine Bedeutung für die Kulturentwicklung in Südwestdeutschland', *Goessler Festschrift*, 168–86.

to south-eastern England, especially to the Thames estuary.[1] Some also lodged themselves in southern Belgium where they were adjacent to the second area of immediate interest.[2] This is the Lower Rhine, and especially those parts of Holland and Belgium west of the Lower Meuse. In all this region the bulk of the population belonged to the Lower Rhenish Urnfield Culture. Intrusive on these sedentary farmers came Hallstatt I warriors, some of whom may have followed the Meuse from Lorraine, but others, and these an important group, appear to have come directly from as far as eastern Bavaria or Bohemia.[3]

Taking the whole Lower Rhenish area into consideration, one finds a bringing together, about the end of the seventh century, of three different branches of the old North Alpine Culture: the oldest settlers being the Urnfielders of the Rhine, the second the West Alpine migrants, and the third, and numerically smallest, the Hallstatt overlords. It is reasonable to assume that they spoke dialects of a common ancestry, and that inter-mingling presented no great difficulties.

The third area for special notice lies quite outside the North Alpine sphere of influence, except in so far as trade, and perhaps horsemen, are concerned. This is the Teutonic zone of the north German plain, Denmark, and the Scandinavian shores of the Baltic. The cultural history of this, the *Nordischer Kreis*,[4] is well known, but two things should be here mentioned. In the first place, the cremation rite had been paramount throughout the later Bronze Age, from Montelius Period III, and this owed much to the great eastern, or Lausitz, Urnfield province centred in Silesia and adjacent parts of Poland. Secondly, it was into this cultural background, in Periods V and VI of Montelius, that there arrived Hallstatt I horse-gear, iron swords, and types of bronze pin. These, as has been noted, came north chiefly by way of the Elbe.

A position has now been reached when the inquiry can be carried over the sea to Scotland.

The undistinguished nature of the final phase of the native Bronze

---

[1] C. F. C. Hawkes (*PPS*, I (1935), 57–59 and (1948), *op. cit.*, 217–18; H. N. Savory (1948), 'The Sword-bearers. A Reinterpretation', *PPS*, XIV (1948), 155–76.

[2] M. E. Mariën, *Oud-Belgie*, Antwerp, 1952.

[3] M. E. Mariën, *Trouvailles du champ d'urnes et des tombelles hallstattiennes de Court-Saint-Etienne*, Brussels, 1958.

[4] C. A. Moberg, *Zonengliederungen der Vorchristlichen Eisenzeit in Nordeuropa*, Lund, 1941.

Age in Scotland, as throughout Britain generally, has been described by Professor Piggott in the last chapter. No well-defined termination can be demonstrated, and only the sparse occurrence of foreign objects, usually in association with native types, bespeak any possible augmentation of the population.

In the following paragraphs little more can be done than to offer a chronological arrangement of the principal finds, and associations, pointing to their external connexions. Already while the native Middle Bronze Age Culture held sway, influences crossed the North Sea from the Nordic region bearing styles in bronze ornaments there at home in Periods late II, and III (Montelius).[1] The appearance and copying of such ornaments is best seen in southern England, but the Glen Trool hoard, from Kirkcudbrightshire, with its twisted bronze wire necklet, or torc, betokens the same trend in Scotland.[2] There is evidence for Nordic influence in Ireland also at this time, witnessed by bronze trumpets and gold ornaments.[3] If the Nordic elements in Ireland and Britain represent no more than trade it is not clear what was obtained in return, but there is no archaeologically satisfying evidence for Nordic settlers at this period. Whatever this 'ornament-horizon' may imply in human activity, the dating of Glen Trool and its congeners would appear to necessitate a position in the twelfth century B.C.

The beginning of the true Late Bronze Age in southern Britain is signified by the introduction of the cut-and-thrust sword, the socketed axe, and the riveted leaf spearhead, c. 1000 B.C. The unassociated scatter of insular types within these categories in Scotland does not on available evidence help the present inquiry, and it is not until the mid and late eighth century B.C. that a new horizon of external contacts can be brought into view. This is represented by the appearance of vessels made in sheet bronze, exemplified by the buckets from Cardross, and Duddingston Loch, which belong to the Irish-British manufactured group defined by Hawkes and Smith, by the small bowls from Ardoe and Balmashanner that are analogous to vessels in the Middle Rhineland, by the bronze bracelets of Covesea type also of Late Urnfield character, and by fittings

[1] M. A. Smith (1959), 'Some Somerset Hoards and their place in the Bronze Age of Southern Britain', *P.P.S*, XXV (1959), 144–87.

[2] V. G. Childe , *The Prehistory of Scotland*, London, 1935, 149.

[3] T. G. E. Powell, 'The Gold Ornament from Mold, Flintshire, North Wales', PPS, XIX (1953), 161–79 for discussion.

for horse-harness and wheeled vehicles.[1] In Scotland these bronze fittings are found in the hoard from Horsehope, Peeblesshire,[2] which stands in close connexion with the hoards from Heathery Burn, Co. Durham, and from Welby, Leicestershire. These, as pointed out by Hawkes and Smith, belong to the Late Urnfield equipment, and not as yet to the types developed by roving Hallstattian overlords. Harness and coach mountings must always have borne a direct relation to horses and vehicles, and these again to people knowledgeable in their employment. It may well be asked if such could have been found amongst the old Bronze Age population, or if horse-driving, at least in this more elaborate style, must not imply newcomers in Scotland no less than in eastern regions south of the Cheviot.

There is another pointer, if at present it be no more, in this direction. Associated with the exotic bronze bracelets, amongst other things, in the cave at Covesea, Moray, and also amongst the complex of finds from the Heathery Burn cave, were potsherds of a plain kind unlike the urn ware of the native Middle Bronze Age.[3] From both sites, amongst sherds of the roughest kind, can be distinguished a rather better-made ware, hard and gritty, and with some angular-shouldered forms. As with the associated really rough flowerpot-shaped vessels, this better ware shows flattened rims, and the unfortunate term 'Flat-Rimmed Pottery' has been applied to the whole assemblage.[4] For the better-quality ware, with angular shoulders, it would be preferable in Scotland to refer to 'Covesea Ware' now that its archaeological setting has been determined with some accuracy. As to the origin of the Covesea-Heathery Burn ceramic type, it must be admitted that insufficient material is as yet available for any sound case to be presented; all that may be said here is that such pottery could well derive from Late Urnfield prototypes along the Rhine, or in the Low Countries. In view of its exotic associations such would be a reasonable possibility, but acceptance of this view would necessarily imply the arrival of settlers on however small a scale. The roughest of the two wares already mentioned has been compared to the *kümmerkeramik* of north-west

[1] C. F. C. Hawkes and M. A. Smith, *op. cit.* (1957), for important discussion of all this material.

[2] S. Piggott, 'A Late Bronze Age Hoard from Peeblesshire', *PSAS*, LXXXVII (1952–53), 175–86.

[3] S. Benton, 'The Excavation of the Sculptor's Cave, Covesea, Morayshire', *PSAS*, LXV (1930–31), 177–216 for original Covesea report. C. F. C. Hawkes and M. A. Smith, *op. cit.* (1957), for discussion and description of Heathery Burn sherds. Their fig. 6 for illustration.

[4] S. Piggott, p. 57 in F. T. Wainwright, ed. *The Problem of the Picts*, 1955.

Germany as distinguished by Sprockhoff.[1] Such an element on the eastern seaboards of Britain need not be discounted, but the fact that at both Covesea and Heathery Burn the users of these pots were obliged to lurk in caves rather suggests an extreme of hard conditions. Had the would-be settlers become fugitives? In any case conditions for making good pottery, in the splendid Rhineland tradition, no longer obtained.

That some bands of colonists, if such they were, fared better than those reduced to cave life is more recently shown by Elizabeth Burley in her important analysis of the metal-work from the excavations at Traprain Law.[2] At Traprain an active Late Bronze Age settlement contemporary with, or little later than, Heathery Burn and Covesea can now be accepted, and skilled excavation will be able to establish the full nature of this occupation. If the evidence now available from Traprain can be filled out, both there and at other sites, a very different complexion for the Celtic settlement of Scotland will be forthcoming than that necessarily sketched here.

From the later part of the seventh century on for another hundred and fifty years all is obscure in Scotland. Mention may be made of the bronze hoard from Adabrock, in the Isle of Lewis, in which the most interesting piece consists of two fragments of a cross-handle bronze bowl of Hallstatt I type.[3] A date c. 600 B.C. for the Adabrock hoard is allowed, but its position, remote other than to western seaways, suggests its journey to Lewis only as an object of barter. It is not until a very late date in the sixth century, or within the beginning of the fifth, that there is again a slight increase in the number of informative finds. To this period belong the hoards from Braes of Gight, Aberdeenshire,[4] and Wester Ord, Ross,[5]

---

[1] E. Sprockhoff, 'Niedersachsens Bedeutung für die Bronzezeit Westeuropas', *Bericht der Römisch-Germanischen Kommission*, XXXI (1941), 1–138, Berlin. C. F. C. Hawkes, 'Britain and N.W. Germany in the Later Bronze Age' in E. Vogt, ed. *Actes de la 3me. Session, Congrés Internat. Préhist. et Protohist. Sciences, Zürich 1950* (Zürich 1953), 227-8.

[2] E. Burley, 'A Catalogue and Survey of the Metal Work from Traprain Law', *PSAS*, LXXXIX (1955–56), 118–226.

[3] J. Anderson, 'Notice of a Hoard of Bronze Implements recently discovered in Lewis', *PSAS*, XLV (1910–11), 27–44. Professor Piggott informs me that the Adabrock fragments most probably belonged to von Merhardt's type B2a. cf. Tf. 3, no. 4. von Merhardt, 'Studien über einige Gattungen von Bronzegefassen', *Römisch-Germanische Zentralmuseums Festschrift*, 11 (1952), 1–71.

[4] G. Muirhead, 'Notice of Bronze Ornaments and a thin Bifid Blade of Bronze from the Braes of Gight, Aberdeenshire', *PSAS*, XXV (1890–91), 135–8.

[5] J. S. Richardson, 'A Hoard of Bronze Objects from Wester Ord, Ross-shire,' *PSAS*, LIX (1924–6).

containing bronze circlets with hanging rings that appear to be in the line of more massive ornaments found in graves of the Hunsrück-Eifel Culture in its earlier phase, which is equivalent to Hallstatt II, or D.[1] Thereafter, in the fifth century B.C., should fall the bronze crooked-neck pins from Tarves, Aberdeenshire, and Orrock, Fife,[2] which possess north-west German analogues. More important for the present question is the pottery from the recently published excavations at Jarlshof in the Shetland Islands.[3] Remote as are these islands, it may be suggested that the Jarlshof sequence, so admirably elucidated by J. R. C. Hamilton, provides a working pilot scheme for the mainland in that the various settlers at Jarlshof had all presumably come north from the mainland. It is perfectly possible that the first settlement at Jarlshof, represented by a cluster of oval 'courtyard' houses enclosed by a wall, and with a hard well-fired pottery, somewhat akin to Covesea ware, should date to the seventh century B.C. The succeeding (Late Bronze 2) settlement, with its large circular houses, its bronze working, and pottery, allied to the wares from Scarborough and All Cannings Cross, may with more certainty be placed in the sixth century B.C. At Jarlshof there is, then, no evidence for change until a new building complex begins with the erection of the broch and its subsidiary structures, and these must belong to the first century A.D. if not later.

For the long centuries between the decline of the Middle Bronze Age Culture of Scotland and the time of troubles connected with the movements of Celtic peoples within the fringes of history, it may be said that an hypothesis exists for thinking that there was some intrusive population in eastern Scotland, whose material culture was of Late Urnfield aspect, and that this event is likely to have taken place at the end of the eighth century B.C. or within the first half of the seventh. These migrants may well, therefore, have spoken a tongue that would be regarded in modern philological terms as Celtic, but whether their social institutions, and their own national or political inclinations would permit these people being called Celts, it is impossible to say.

To understand the trend of events which finally brought large numbers of Celtic migrants to Scotland, it is convenient to revert to the Celts of

[1] K. Tackenberg, *op. cit.* (1954), 56, for bibl. Specimens from Heimbach and Gladbach are in the museum at Neuwied. [2] *Brit. Mus. Guide Antiqs. Bronze Age* (1920), fig. 105; Cicely M. Piggott 'A late Bronze Age Burial from Orrock near Burntisland', *PSAS*, LXXXII (1947–48), 306–8. [3] J. R. C. Hamilton, *Excavations at Jarlshof, Shetland*, Edinburgh, 1956.

the Middle Rhine, in the mid and late fifth century B.C., where the rich chariot graves betoken a barbarian aristocracy, the early patrons of the La Tène art style, and, with little doubt, the instigators to some degree of the Celtic Migration Period evidenced south of the Alps, within the literate world, by the establishment of Cisalpine Gaul, and the incursions to the Balkans and Asia Minor.[1]

There remained, of course, no tradition of the new deployment of power, with its consequent adoption of La Tène cultural elements, amongst the tribes from Gaul to Bohemia, or from the Swiss Lakes to the Channel. The expansion of the La Tène warriors of the Middle Rhine may have been an urgent reason for large-scale migrations to Britain, in the early or mid-fifth century B.C., bringing over people with a late and provincial Hallstatt Culture, and coming perhaps mainly from north-eastern France, but again also from the Lower Rhenish area. These new-comers were the creators of the British Iron Age A Culture, and they must be regarded as having formed the bulk of the Celtic population in Britain from thenceforward.[2] In due course, however, an intrusion, or a number of small landings, of La Tène warriors took place, and the outcome is manifest in the numerous hill-top defences put up by the settled inhabitants, by some few strongholds of the invaders, together with their novel metal and ceramic forms, but especially by the appearance of fine metal-work in the La Tène style for the adornment of the warrior, his horses and chariot.[3] The chariot graves of such warriors are known principally from a group in east Yorkshire, although they are sadly impoverished as compared with those of their forebears on the Middle Rhine, or in Champagne.[4]

The date of the La Tène intrusions, forming the British Iron Age 'B' Culture, is generally considered to lie within the first half of the third century B.C., and it may well be that in bringing over the ancient funeral rite, and the tradition of heroic overlordship with its attendant luxury crafts, these anonymous Celtic chieftains ensured for many centuries the

[1] Summarized by A. Grenier, *Les Gaulois*, Paris, 1945, 107–26, and by T. G. E. Powell, *op. cit.* (1958).

[2] C. F. C. Hawkes, 'The ABC of the British Iron Age', *Antiquity* XXXIII (1958), 170–82.

[3] J. M. de Navarro, 'The Celts in Britain and their Art', *The Heritage of Early Britain*, 56–82, London, 1952. But see now E. M. Jope, 69–83 in S. S. Frere, ed. *Problems of the Iron Age in Southern Britain*, London, 1961.

[4] As illustrated by P. Jacobsthal, *Early Celtic Art*, Oxford, 1944.

continuation in these islands of their social and cultural heritage. Their zenith on the European mainland had already been reached.

Again, for Scotland, it is unfortunately still impossible to say to what degree these La Tène Celtic migrants contributed to its peoplement. No monuments or domestic material can be attributed to them, but there is the outstanding find of fine metal-work from Torrs, near Castle Douglas, Kirkcudbrightshire. The find consisted of an ornamental bronze cap for a pony's head, and the bronze terminals for a pair of drinking-horns.

These important objects have received recent detailed study.[1] They are representative of an early stage in the style of insular La Tène art, incorporating plastic and surface decorative motifs, and they have been given an approximate date early within the second half of the third century B.C. The finding of the Torrs objects in a peat bog, once probably a sheet of open water, suggests that they formed part of a votive offering. This deduction might lead to a further inference that the find spot was the sacred pool of a locally resident community, but it might also suggest, as in the case of the great votive deposit at Llyn Cerrig Bach in Anglesey,[2] that the objects had been brought from a distance, and in this case offered when the owners were about to embark for Ireland. While this might help to explain the presence of such fine pieces of Celtic craftsmanship in so isolated a region, it would also have to be supposed that the objects were old when offered to the supernatural, for the Irish archaeological evidence does not seem to provide for a date earlier than the first century B.C. for the arrival of chieftains or craftsmen bearing this art style.[3] The Celtic peoplement of Ireland has, like that of Scotland, to be considered in relation to the course of events during the early first century B.C. in Gaul and southern Britain. Here only the situation in southern Britain need be touched upon, but the establishment of Belgic kingdoms in the south-east, together with penetrations farther north, even to the Humber, provide at least one adequate explanation for large-scale intrusions of dispossessed tribes across the Pennines and Cheviots.

The disruptions caused by the Belgae, and in little more than a century

---

[1] R. J. C. Atkinson and S. Piggott, 'The Torrs Chamfrein', *Archaeologia*, XCVI (1955), 197–235.

[2] C. Fox, *A Find of the Early Iron Age from Llyn Cerrig Bach, Anglesey*, Cardiff, 1946.

[3] R. J. C. Atkinson and S. Piggott, *op. cit.* (1955), 231–5; E. M. Jope, 'An Iron Age Decorated Sword-Scabbard from the River Bann at Toome', *UJA*, XVII (1954–55), 81–91 states a case for earlier dating.

later by the Roman invasion of Britain,[1] bring Scotland fully within the pattern of insular Celtic settlement. The hillforts and other strongholds, which might have been expected to fill out the archaeological record for the centuries in which the Iron Age Cultures of southern Britain had dedeveloped, are found, on the evidence of recent studies, to be of no greater antiquity than this final prehistoric phase. The matter has been fully discussed in recent publications,[2] but a sketch must here be attempted in order to conclude the chapter with a clearly defined population of Celticspeaking tribes in Scotland.

The hill-forts, brochs, and fortified homesteads of various kinds, from whose scant domestic debris a beginning not earlier than the first century B.C. must be deduced, form the witnesses for a very considerable overrunning of Scotland by dispossessed Celtic tribes from the more vulnerable regions of Britain south of the Cheviots. The possibility that refugees from western Gaul also sought sanctuary must not be forgotten. This may be especially the case in the Western Isles,[3] but in general the weight of testimony speaks for purely insular movements.

On the basis of geography and types of stronghold, but not on any clear picture of domestic crafts, it seems possible to define three main provinces established in Scotland, by the middle of the first century A.D., on the threshold of the Agricolan campaigns. North of the Great Glen dwelt the inhabitants of the brochs, concentrated in Caithness and Sutherland as well as in Orkney, Shetland, and, on the west coast, in Skye.[4] A scatter of these 'tower-houses' existed in the Lowlands probably representing individual enterprises. The second province may be called that of the vitrified forts, as these are the most easily distinguishable members of a type of hill-top stronghold with walls constructed in dry masonry with timber lacings. The result of conflagration of the timberwork, intentional or accidental, caused the fusing of the surrounding stone, and this therefore cannot be regarded as an absolute distinguishing feature. These forts are distributed at either end of the Great Glen, around the Firth of Clyde, with outliers in Galloway, and in Angus and

[1] I. A. Richmond, *Roman Britain*, London, 1955.

[2] S. Piggott in Wainwright, F. T., ed. *op. cit.* (1955), 66–86.

[3] L. S. Scott, 'Gallo-British Colonies. The Aisled Roundhouse Culture in the North', *PPS*, XIV (1948), 46—125.

[4] L. S. Scott, 'The Problem of the Brochs', *PPS*, XIII (1947), 1–36. A. Graham, 'Some Observations on the Brochs', *PSAS*, LXXXI (1946–47), 48–99.

Fife with other eastern outliers.[1] The third, and most recently distinguished, province is that of the dense concentration of small hill-top forts, of various but interrelated constructional techniques, found on the hills of the Border country, especially overlooking the drainage area of the Tweed.[2]

On general considerations an hypothesis may be formed that the vitrified forts should represent the first and most formidable of the first century B.C. Celtic intrusions, taking over the best territory, and controlling the principal maritime entries and land routes. As compared with the defensive works of the other provinces, these vitrified forts speak for close continuity with the building traditions of the larger hill-forts of the British Iron Age 'A' Culture, and, behind that, the continental Hallstatt stone and timber fortifications. It might appear that this strongly held central part of Scotland had obliged the migrant communities, who later built the brochs, to move so far north to find an area for rehabilitation. At about the same time the Border country became overcrowded owing to this same barrier lying to its north, and the ever-growing menace of Roman arms to the south.

This matter may throw some further light on the motive of the Orkney chieftains who, as reported by Orosius, travelled south to submit to Claudius.[3] Piggott has shown that there exists the inference that the Orcadians knew the appropriate procedure for gaining Roman friendship from earlier contact previous to their migration.[4] It must be presumed on this basis that the Orcadians had some immediate advantage to hope for in this alliance, and their particular concern is likely to have lain along their southern frontier, where better lands were held by a hostile power. If this was the Orcadian diplomacy, it was quite in line with that of Celtic tribes elsewhere, both in Britain and Gaul, who had grievances against neighbours. Roman arms never, as things turned out, reached sufficiently far north to assist the Orcadians; if such, in fact, was the intention on either side.

The people of the vitrified forts are likely to have been dispossessed

[1] R. W. Feachem, 'Fortifications' in Wainwright, F. T., ed. *op. cit.* (1955), 66–86, for discussion of fortifications and distribution map of brochs and vitrified forts.

[2] S. Piggott, 'Prehistoric Settlement' in *Scientific Survey of S.E. Scot.* (Brit. Assoc.) (1951), 44–53 and fig. 9.

[3] V. G. Childe, *Scotland Before the Scots*, London, 1946, 129.

[4] S. Piggott in Wainwright, F. T., ed. *op. cit.* (1955), 59.

of their territories south of the Antonine Wall, but much remained to them to the north of it, and especially valuable would have been the east coast plain and its river valleys between the Firth of Forth and the Moray Firth. Here would seem to have continued the hard core of native resistance, and it is in just this region that the Picts emerge in post-Roman times. Here, too, is the surviving concentration of place-name elements which Jackson has most recently discussed, and has shown to belong to a form of Celtic related to, but not identical with, the language of the Britons as spoken throughout most of the island in Roman times.[1]

The Gallo-Brittonic dialect deduced by Jackson as having been spoken within this subsequent Pictish territory may very reasonably be assigned, as he has suggested, to the vitrified-fort people. To seek an alternative identity is to raise greater difficulties, and the very fact of the survival of this dialect, however mixed with an indigenous non-Indo-European element it may have been, presupposes a political and social foundation of sufficient strength to withstand a long period of strife, and eventual re-emergence as a political entity in early historical times.[2]

The virtual absence of Gallo-Brittonic type place-names in the vitrified-fort regions of the west and south-west may be explained as the result of comprehensive repopulation. South of the Antonine Wall, in the future territory of the Strathclyde 'Welsh', it would presumably have been Roman policy to establish client tribes from the adjacent British-speaking territories.

North of the Antonine Wall, and between the Clyde and the Firth of Lorne, the linguistic position may well have remained unaltered until the Irish plantations, culminating in the establishment of the kingdom of Dalriada in the fifth century A.D.[3] Surprising as it may at first appear, it was this event that brought to Scotland the Gaelic branch of Celtic, and with it the whole legacy of Celtic institutional survivals that continued into medieval times.

It is an excellent object lesson in the complexities of the study of national origins that Gaelic, the most archaic of the known Celtic languages, should have been the latest to take root in Scotland,[4] but both the question of

[1] K. H. Jackson, 'The Pictish Language', in Wainwright, F. T., ed. *op. cit.*, (1955), 129–60.
[2] F. T. Wainwright, 'The Picts and the Problem' in Wainwright, F. T., ed. (1955).
[3] H. M. Chadwick, *Early Scotland*, Cambridge, 1949.
[4] K. H. Jackson, 'Common Gaelic', *Prov. Brit. Acad.*, XXXVII (1951), 71–97.

Gaelic origins in Ireland[1] and the fortunes of the Dalriadic Scots lie beyond the terms of this chapter.

[1] T. F. O'Rahilly, *Early Irish History and Mythology*, Dublin, 1946; T. G. E. Powell, 'The Celtic Settlement of Ireland' 173–95 in Fox and Dickins, ed. *The Early Cultures of North-West Europe* (*H.M. Chadwick Essays*), Cambridge, 1950. The author considers this to have been only a provisional statement on a problem still far from solution.

CHAPTER FIVE

From Prehistory to History

MODERN Scotland has arisen from the union of five known peoples. The process, which covers the period from the ninth to the fifteenth century, is recorded in historical documents and will be briefly noted as the individual peoples are discussed. Of these peoples two—the Angles and the Norse—were Teutonic speaking; they arrived in the country between the end of the Roman period (c. A.D. 400) and the establishment of feudalism in the twelfth century. The Angles, firmly established in the richest part of the Lowlands and sharing the heritage of their wealthier and more numerous kinsmen south of the modern Border, gradually asserted a preponderant influence on the cultural and linguistic destiny of the country, which had earlier been dominated by the Goidelic-speaking Scots. This people, or at least the ruling element, was also a late arrival, coming from Ireland; the problem of its settlement in Argyll is complicated by traditions of earlier invasions from the same country, traditions that find a certain confirmation in the archaeological record. Celtic speaking like the Scots, but belonging to the Brittonic branch of that family, the Britons and Picts were older immigrants. Both were firmly established in modern Scotland before the period of the Roman invasions; their arrival must be dated to the prehistoric age, probably within the final half-millennium before our era. The Romans, representing, in their contacts with the north, a political system rather than a people, need not be considered in the present context, though their culture and statecraft profoundly influenced the development of the older peoples. Beyond these five groups, who figure in the historical record, there are fleeting glimpses of older peoples, who must either remain nameless or whose names are a matter of conjecture; some of them probably figure in the classical records, but they had ceased to exist as separate groups when the medieval documentation becomes extensive and trustworthy in the course of the twelfth century. The task set in the present chapter is to examine the information relating to each of the known groups, in order to see how far it is possible to correlate the historical and linguistic record with the material data supplied by archaeology. Such a correlation must rely largely on distribution maps, a method of presenting evidence that is equally useful in dealing with data from any source.

At this point a preliminary caution on some of the classes of material available would seem to be indicated. The archaeological data follow on from those used in the earlier chapters and no special technique is required. The written record is a new development. When first available it is very scanty. The few scraps of information that chance has preserved for modern study do not present a coherent picture. They are odd facts, taken from works compiled for various purposes. They must always be interpreted in relation to the original purpose for which the document was compiled; in particular it must be emphasized that, down to the twelfth century, when this survey ends, the bulk of the available material is never sufficiently great to establish a negative. Moreover, much of the written evidence is preserved in ecclesiastical sources of a much later date. The technical criticism of these sources is a specialized science; any attempt to use the information drawn from them must take account of the historical limitations of these writings and the circumstances of their composition and transmission. The linguistic material, largely embodied in the toponymy of the medieval Scotland, is also a specialized study, from which general historical conclusions are only now beginning to emerge. Too facile use of this material in the past has led to much confusion of thought and faulty deductions that have served to bring discredit on to a number of students of prehistory.

Addressing a learned public, it should be unnecessary to add one particular caution. Modern political thought often tends to regard language as an innate inherent possession of a people, something that enshrines its traditions and its very being. Historically language has, on occasion, changed without any essential alteration in the physical composition of a people. In 1650 Ireland, outside the English Pale round

Dublin, was Gaelic speaking; three centuries later the Gaeltacht has shrunk to a few scattered enclaves in the south and west. This change has been effected by an immigrant aristocracy—the Protestant Ascendancy— few in numbers, but for long the only repository of political power and material wealth. The replacement of the early speeches—Celtic and others—by the Romance tongues of France, Italy, and Spain during the 450 years of Roman rule is another example. Not every mingling of peoples has resulted in a similar sweeping change, but the possibility of such a change is one which must be taken into account when using linguistic evidence.

The Angles (fig. 14)

The Anglo-Saxon lands between the Forth and the Tweed were ceded to King Kenneth II after a meeting at Chester in 973. The arrangement was made as part of an attempt by the Anglo-Saxon ruler, Edgar, to regulate relations with his northern neighbours and to secure the allegiance of the Scottish king.[1] These lands were an old Anglian possession and had formed part of the kingdom of Northumbria for nearly four centuries. They were Anglo-Saxon in speech and had been the homeland of many famous Northumbrians, including St. Cuthbert, who spent his youth as a shepherd on the banks of the Leader. Melrose and Coldingham were Northumbrian monasteries, indistinguishable from Lindisfarne and Whitby.

The area ceded in 973 included most of the modern Lothians and the greater part of the basin of the Tweed. At an earlier date, before the disturbances occasioned by the Scandinavian invasions and settlements on the shores of the Solway (p. 135), Northumbrian rule had extended more widely north of the later Border. Whithorn, in the far west of Galloway, was already a Northumbrian bishopric when Bede wrote his Ecclesiastical History of the English People in 731.[2] It was still Northumbrian when the monks of Lindisfarne arrived about 880, with the relics saved from the Danish sack of their own monastery.[3] Kyle in Ayrshire had

---

[1] F. M. Stenton, Anglo-Saxon England, 365; A. O. Anderson, Early Sources of Scottish History, 478.

[2] Bedae Historia ecclesiastica, v, 23; Dumfriesshire and Galloway Natural History and Antiquarian Society (cited as DGNHAS) Trans., III, xxvii, 95.

[3] Symeonis monachi Historia Dunelmensis Ecclesiae, ii, 12 (Rolls Series, lxxv, i, 67); DGNHAS Trans., III, xxvii, 96.

been conquered in 750[1] and, at the end of the previous century, Ecgfrith, the Northumbrian king, had taken the offensive against the Pictish lands north of the Forth, until he met his death at Nechtansmere (685). His wide supremacy in the north did not survive that disaster, but the Forth seems to have remained the northern frontier of Anglian Northumbria.[2]

Monumental sculpture provides the principal archaeological check on the expansion of Northumbrian power. Crosses like those at Ruthwell[3] and Hoddom[4] in Dumfriesshire, or Aberlady[5] and Abercorn[6] in the Lothians, are as Anglian in spirit and in execution as those south of the modern Border; the Scottish Lowlands provide an appreciable proportion of the finest Northumbrian sculpture of the early period. In this area there must have been a real immigration, transforming the racial composition of the people. Farther west Anglian influence can be seen in a few of the early monuments of Galloway; Whithorn nos. 3 and 5 are examples. The influence here is political and perhaps less deeply rooted, but the reality of the penetration cannot be doubted. Passing north of the Forth, Anglian influence is again apparent in the monuments; but Anglian motives, such as the vine scroll, normally appear in combination with native themes, such as the Pictish symbol—Hilton of Cadboll in Ross-shire, dating from about 800, may serve as an example of this hybrid art, which need indicate no settlement by an alien people.

The date of the Anglian advance into modern Scotland lies in the years around A.D. 600. About that date Morgan Mwynfawr, a British ruler, whose seat (Eiddyn) was perhaps at Edinburgh, perhaps at Dalmahoy on the Pentlands, is commemorated in the early Welsh poem of Aneirin (p. 139). There were pagan Angles near Hoddom on the Annan about the same time or a little earlier, though the country was still under the rule of a British king.[7] In the last quarter of the sixth century Anglian rule was not yet firmly established in the north; the British kings were strong

---

[1] *Bedae continuatio,* s.a. 750.

[2] *The Problem of the Picts,* 7–8, for details and references.

[3] G. Baldwin Brown, *The Arts in Early England,* v, 305–17.

[4] *DGNHAS Trans.,* III, xxxi, 174–97.

[5] A. W. Clapham, *English Romanesque Architecture before the Conquest,* 64, pl. 13.

[6] *ibid.,* 64, pl. 14; the exact date 681–5, postulated on historical grounds, cannot be justified.

[7] *Vita Kentigerni,* cap. xxxii; the life dates from the twelfth century, but is based on earlier sources; the reference to Woden in this passage indicates an earlier written source.

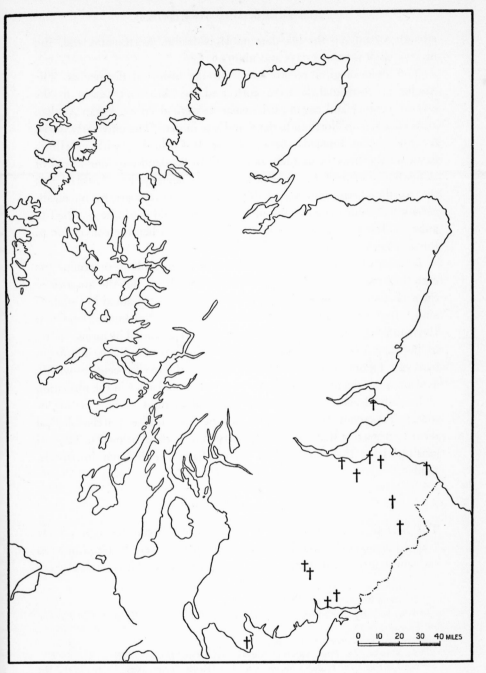

Fig. 14. Anglian-type Crosses (650–850).

enough to shut up the invaders on Holy Island, Northumberland, and besiege them for three days and nights.[1]

The archaeological record bears out the historical documents. The Angles or Northumbria were converted to Christianity early in the seventh century and pagan burial customs were given up. Pagan Anglian graves are few in Northumberland and late in date. The only early burial recorded is an isolated woman's grave at Corbridge, with cruciform brooches that may be as early as *c*. 500.[2] In Scotland only one burial of pagan Saxon character is known, a grave at Dalmeny, East Lothian, and the Northumbrian affinities of this isolated discovery are by no means certain.[3] On this evidence the invasion of Scotland could be ascribed to a date as late as or later than the period 600–25, when the conversion to the new faith took place.

In the absence of a detailed survey it is not possible to determine the early incidence of Anglian place-names in Scotland. But the absence of the early type of name ending in -ing or -ingas has been noted in Cumberland.[4] Both there and east of the Pennines, in Northumberland and Durham[5], the oldest stratum of place-names is represented by forms ending in -ingaham, which also occur rarely in southern Scotland (e.g. Tinningaham and Tigbrethingham, both preserved in the twelfth-century writer, Symeon of Durham).[6] These forms represent an old stage in the formation of English place-names, but one not so old as those ending in -ing or -ingas. Toponymy therefore confirms the historical and archaeological record, suggesting that the Anglian entry into Scotland belongs to a period sensibly later than the primary Anglo-Saxon settlements in eastern England.

The Norse (*figs. 15 and 16*)

The Scandinavian impact on western Europe began through piracy. Wealthy monasteries like Lindisfarne and Jarrow were being plundered and burnt in the last decade of the eighth century. These attacks were

[1] Stenton, *op. cit.*, 74–77.

[2] Baldwin Brown, *op. cit.*, iv, 811.

[3] *Proc. Soc. Ant. Scot.*, xlix, 332–8; *R. Comm. Hist. Mons.: Mid- and West Lothian*, no. 340.

[4] *English Place Name Survey*, xxii, p. xxi.

[5] A. Mawer, *The Place Names of Northumberland and Durham*, xvii.

[6] *Symeonis monachi Historia Regum*, s.a. 854 (Rolls Series, lxxv, ii, 101); the list from which these names are taken is probably as old as the tenth century.

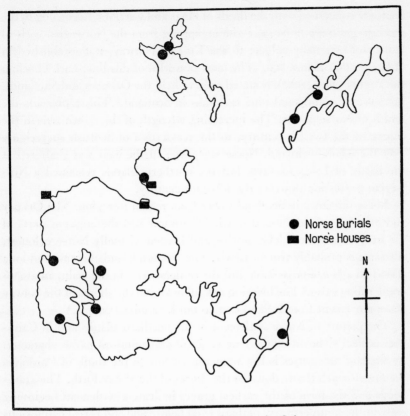

Fig. 15. Norse Burials and houses in Orkney.

soon followed by settlement. Dicuil, the Irishman, writing in *c.* 825, records that the Celtic hermits from Ireland had deserted the Faerøe Islands because of the molestation of the Norsemen.[1] This is evidence of a search after new lands for settlement, as this remote community can hardly have held out the prospect of loot. The Irish annals note the sack of Iona early in the ninth century,[2] and it is likely that the wealthier monasteries in Scotland were attacked little later than those of England and Ireland.

The beginning of Norse settlement in the area of modern Scotland is less easy to follow in the sources. The native chronicles, English or Irish, are mainly interested in ecclesiastical history, while the Scandinavian

[1] *Dicuili liber de Mensura Orbis Terrae*, cap. vii.
[2] *Annals of Ulster*, s.a. 801 (ed. Hennessy, i, 286).

sagas are concerned with the deeds of kings and warriors. According to the *Orkneyinger Saga*, a Norse earldom, sprung from the Norwegian earls of Møre and nominally subject to the King of Norway, was established in Orkney rather before 900.[1] The most powerful of this line, Earl Thorfinn the Mighty (*ob. c.* 1065), is stated to have held the Orkneys and Shetlands, the western islands and nine earldoms in Scotland.[2] This represents the zenith of Norse power. The increasing strength of the crown led, in the course of the twelfth century, to the reassertion of Scottish sovereignty over the whole mainland. Norse sea power in the west was shattered at the battle of Largs in 1263, but the northern islands remained a Norwegian possession down to the fifteenth century.

Norse influence in Scotland varies from region to region. The Orkney and Shetland islands, together with Caithness and the adjacent parts of the mainland, were thickly settled and became virtually Norse colonies; the same is probably true of Lewis. The western islands became and long remained a Norse possession, but the settlers were, in the main, an aristocratic ruling caste.[3] The invasion of Galloway and the shores of the Solway was a movement from Ireland carried out by a mixed people.[4]

The picture of Norse settlement in the northern islands and in Caithness is clearly shown by the long series of grave finds of pagan character. In Shetland this series is less numerous, while to the south of Caithness the finds stretch thinly down to the shores of the Moray Firth. The grave-goods and the form of the earliest graves indicate a settlement beginning early in the ninth century, perhaps even before 800 and reveal connexions with west Norway, and in particular with the provinces of Møre, Rogaland, and Trondelag.[5] The area covered is that for which there is historical evidence of activity by the early Norse earls, but the series begins nearly a hundred years before the recorded foundation of the dynasty (p. 130). In particular the extension of the graves down to the Moray Firth is borne out by the *Saga* record of the death of Earl Sigurd in this area and his burial in a howe on the banks of the Oykel, which now forms the southern boundary of Sutherland.[6]

[1] *The Earl's Saga*, cap. 4 (Rolls Series, lxxxviii, iii, 4–5).

[2] *ibid.*, cap. 38 (p. 59).

[3] For this contrast cf. A. W. Brøgger, *Ancient Emigrants*, 126–7.

[4] *English Place Name Survey: Cumberland* (vol. xxii, p. xxiii–xxvii).

[5] Brøgger, *op. cit.*, ch. IV and appendix; cf. *R. Comm. Hist. Mon.: Orkney and Shetland*, i, 24–26; Scientific Research Fund of 1919, *Viking Remains in British Isles.*

[6] *The Earl's Saga*, cap 5 (Rolls Series, lxxxviii, iii, 6).

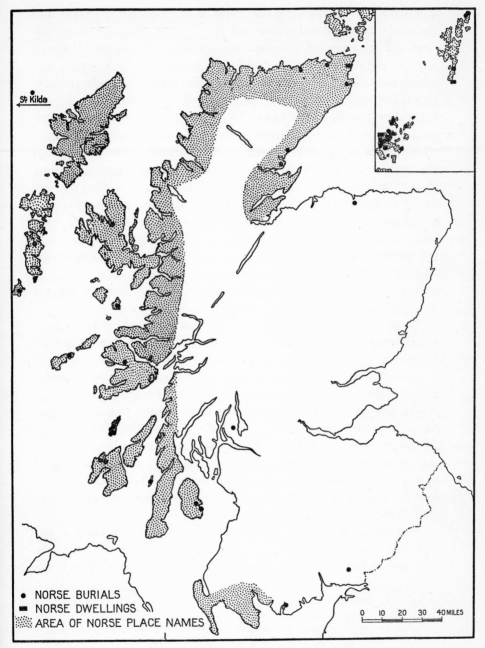

St. Kilda

● NORSE BURIALS
▬ NORSE DWELLINGS
▦ AREA OF NORSE PLACE NAMES

0 10 20 30 40 MILES

Fig. 16. Norse settlement in Scotland.

Place-names tell the same story. The older toponymy of Orkney and Shetland is predominantly Norse and derived from western Norway. The same elements recur in Caithness and penetrate as far as the Beauly Firth.[1] The place-name evidence is largely concerned with farm names, and recent excavations have shown that the farm types of the oldest Norse period in Orkney and Shetland are typical of the earliest stage of Norse colonial penetration to Iceland in the ninth century. The long rectangular dwelling with the sides bowed outwards and the turf, stone-faced walls which appear in the earliest Norse farms at Jarlshof, on the Mainland of Shetland, find their best analogies in Iceland.[2] The same type of dwelling is also known at Birsay, on the Mainland of Orkney, at a period that can hardly be later than the ninth century; there these farms antedate the Earl's Hall, of which there is at least one stage older than the eleventh century rebuild attributed to Earl Thorfinn the Mighty.[3] Similar farms are known at Freswick in Caithness,[4] but these resemble in detail the later Norse farms of the islands.

The settlement in the north, including Caithness, brought about a complete change of language and, in all probability, a considerable change in the population. The old Norse laws, in particular the odal rights in land, survived with modifications until the modern period, and the local Norse dialect, the Norn, was still used in the islands in the eighteenth century. The only other area in which there is evidence for a similar change is the island of Lewis, which is thought to have been entirely Norse speaking in the eleventh century.[5] 'The Lewis Gaelic', to quote Oftedal, 'in many respects stands apart from all the neighbouring dialects. . . .' All Gaelic names are relatively modern in appearance and very many of them (perhaps between fifty and eighty per cent) are automatically dated as post Norse by the Norse elements they contain.' The relevant archaeological record from the island is too scanty to provide a basis for any deduction.[6]

Norse place-names occur throughout the western islands down to and including Arran. They are also found along the whole west coast of the mainland, as far as the Mull of Kintyre. The proportion is highest in the

[1] Brøgger, *op. cit.*, ch. III.
[2] J. R. C. Hamilton, *Jarlshof*, 93–95.
[3] Official Guide (Ministry of Works).
[4] *Proc. Soc. Ant. Scot.*, lxxiii, 71–109; lxxvii, 5–16.
[5] Oftedal in *Annen Viking Kongress*, Bergen, 1953, 107–12.
[6] *R. Comm. Hist. Mons.: The Outer Hebrides and Skye*, liv.

Outer Hebrides, but, except in Lewis, there is no reason to suppose that Norse speech entirely supplanted the local Gaelic.[1] Norse archaeological remains in this area include a considerable number of rich burials and occasional articles of luxury. Ship burials with coins of Archbishop Wigmund of York (831–54) are recorded on the islands of Canna[2] and Colonsay.[3] A ship burial was also found on Oronsay[4] and the presence of boat rivets in the burial mound at Kingscross on Arran[5] points to a further grave of that type. The rich ship burial indicates a man of high rank, a chieftain; it is not typical. But even the ordinary Norse burials on the western islands, such as the secondary interment in the mound at Tote, Skeabost, on Skye,[6] or that at Ardvourney on Barra,[7] are those of men of some standing, not peasant settlers. Some corroboration of the aristocratic character and numerically small numbers of the settlers in the west is afforded by the ecclesiastical organization. The landowner's small chapel—correlated in Orkney with the ounceland, or Norse taxation unit, and in Man with the treen—also appears in the west. While in Orkney these dedications show little or no trace of Celtic practice, a survey of the similar evidence in Islay reveals the continuity of the Celtic pattern of dedications. Evidence of this type has not been studied in detail and it is at present impossible to do more that record the impression that the Christian communities of the west, though harried by the Norse attacks, managed to survive through the period of the raids, while Christianity in the far north was introduced anew in the eleventh century.

The Norse invasion of Galloway and the Solway shores was part of a wider movement which set Raegnald on the throne of York in 919. Raegnald belonged to the Norwegian dynasty of Dublin.[8] The invasion along the Solway coasts must have taken place in the years preceding the conquest of York, and the Durham records afford a glimpse of the confusion reigning in these years and of the flight of Anglian landholders eastward across the mountains.[9]

---

[1] Oftedal, *op. cit.*, 109.

[2] *R. Comm. Hist. Monts.: The Outer Hebrides and Skye*, no. 686.

[3] *Proc. Soc. Ant. Scot.*, xli, 443–9.

[4] *ibid.*, 437–41.

[5] *ibid.*, xliii, 371–5.

[6] *Arch. Journ.*, lxxvii, 135–6.

[7] *Proc. Soc. Ant. Lond.*, II, ii, 229–31.

[8] F. M. Stenton, *Anglo-Saxon England*, 328–30; cf. *R. Comm. Hist. Mons.: Westmorland*, xlviii–l.

[9] *Historia de Sancto Cuthberto*, 22–23 (Rolls Series, lxxv, i, 208–9).

The settlement in Galloway is marked by the Irish-Norse place-names, which cover much of Wigtownshire and the coasts of Kirkcudbrightshire and Dumfriesshire. The settlers were already Christian or partly Christian and the area occupied is further defined by the Anglo-Norse type of sculptured crosses, of which the most numerous and most characteristic belong to the Whithorn school. These crosses have a wheel head and interlacing ornaments, which is based on older Anglian motives, adapted to suit the more barbaric taste of the new rulers.[1]

The Scots

The Scots of Argyll, whose ruler, Kenneth Mac Alpin, became King of the Picts in the middle of the ninth century, were Goidelic speaking and of Irish origin. In early usage the words Scoti and Scotia meant Irish and Ireland.[2] At the end of the sixth century the ruler of the Scots was Aedh, son of Gabran, who had been ordained king by St. Columba.[3] He was a powerful and aggressive warrior, but his campaigns ended in defeats, by the Picts in the battle of Circinn, perhaps in the Mearns, and by the Northumbrians at Degsastan, probably in Liddesdale. Aedh, who belonged to the line of Knapdale, was a great-grandson of Fergus, who 'was the first of the race of Conaire to take the kingdom of Alban from the mountain of Druimalban to the Irish Sea and the Isles of the Gael'.[4] His death occurred about 500 and he is stated to have reigned three years. The same tradition identified Conaire as Conaire mac Moga Lama, one of the Ernean rulers of Munster. A rather older source, the Duan Albanach, gives a variant version:

> The three sons of Erc, son of Eochaidh, the valiant,
> Three who obtained the blessing of Patrick,
> took Alban, exalted their courage,
> Loarn, Feargus and Angus.

---

[1] *DGNHAS, Trans.*, III, vii, 97–117.

[2] e.g. *Adamnani vita Columbae*, praef. ii: de Scotia in Britanniam of St. Columba coming to Iona, and ii. 46: Pictorum plebe et Scotorum Britanniae.

[3] *ibid.*, iii, 5.

[4] *Chronicle of the Scots* (W. F. Skene, *Chronicles of the Picts*, 130), a twelfth-century MS. which contains the traditions of the Scots of Argyll. For the death of Fergus see *Annals of Tighernagh* at a date which should probably be equated to A.D. 501 (*Rev. celt.*, xvii, 124).

To Loarn is attributed a reign of ten years in Scotland, followed by twenty-seven years' rule of his brother Fergus.[1] If the death of Fergus in *c.* 500 is correct, this would imply the establishment of the dynasty in the third quarter of the fifth century. The apostle of Argyll, St. Columba, founded the monastery at Iona in 563; he was the son of Fedilmidh mac Fergus, a great-grandson of Nial of the Nine Hostages, who was responsible for the establishment in Ulster of the rule of the Goidelic dynasty of Tara.[2]

The Scots of Argyll were Goidelic in speech and the term 'common Gaelic' has been coined to denote the language used both there and in Ireland. As a result of ecclesiastical influence, based on Iona, this language had probably made some penetration into the Pictish area before the union of the kingdom in the middle of the ninth century; this union led to a great extension of the area of Goidelic speech.[3] At the moment of its greatest extension, in the eleventh century, Gaelic was in use throughout the whole of modern Scotland, except for a small strip along the English Border and the Norse-speaking areas in the north and in Lewis.[4] Already, in the tenth century, the languages spoken in Scotland and in Ireland had begun to diverge, though the basic unity of the sea-divided Gael survived, at least sentimentally, down to the destruction of Irish Gaelic culture in the seventeenth century.

The archaeological evidence for early connexions between Argyll and Ireland is slight. The oldest inscriptions of Iona[5] find their closest parallels on Irish sites like Clonmacnoise,[6] but they stand alone. The ascription of the Book of Kells to Iona[7] has yet to be proved. The manuscripts, in any case, are a common expression of ecclesiastical art, in which Iona probably acted as the link between the churches of Ireland and of Anglian Northumbria. The Ogam inscriptions afford stronger evidence of the spread of Irish influences. The alphabet was brought to Argyll as part of the cultural heritage of the invaders. From there it spread into the Pictish areas in the course of the eighth century; it was there used for

[1] Skene, *Chronicles of the Picts*, 59.

[2] T. F. O'Rahilly, *Early Irish History and Mythology*, 209–34.

[3] K. Jackson in *Proc. Brit. Acad.*, xxxvii, 71–97.

[4] Oftedal, *op. cit.*, 109.

[5] J. Romilly Allen, *Early Christian Monuments of Scotland*, 398–400.

[6] R. A. S. Macalister, *The Memorial Slabs of Clonmacnois*, 102; Iona no. 4 is typologically earlier than the series ascribed to the eighth century.

[7] F. Masai, *Les Origines de la Miniature irlandaise*, 122–4; but see E. A. Lowe, *Codices Latini Antiquiores*, ii, no. 274.

memorials, bearing Pictish names.[1] A similar development has been postulated for the boss style on the later crosses. This is found in Ireland, in Argyll, and in the Pictish area of Scotland, and could be regarded as the result of cultural influences spreading with the new rulers of the Picts after the union of the kingdom in the ninth century. But neither the sequence nor the dating of these monuments is firmly established and a discussion of the problems involved would be out of place in the present context.[2]

The Britons

The cession of Strathclyde to King Malcolm I of Scotland is recorded in the Anglo-Saxon Chronicle under the year 945. This amounted to no more than a cession of the supremacy and the old native dynasty survived into the early eleventh century in the person of Owain.[3] The earlier descent of this line is recorded in the old Welsh genealogy in Harley Ms. 3857, a twelfth-century source copying an original drawn up in the middle of the tenth century at the court of Owain ap Hywel Dda of Dyfed.[4] Allowing the normal thirty years to a generation, a scale checked in this case by annalistic references, these rulers can be traced back to the first half of the fifth century.

Floruit	*Harley* 3857, *pedigree v*	*Annalistic references*[5]
890–920	Run	
860–890	son of Arthgal	Arthgal king of the Britons of Srath Cluaide . . . killed (*AU:* 871).
830–860	son of Dumnagual	
800–830	son of Riderch	
770–800	son of Eugein	
740–770	son of Dumnagual	Dumnagual son of Teudubr dies (*AC:* 760).

[1] K. Jackson in *The Problem of the Picts*, 139–42.

[2] C. A. Ralegh Radford in *Antiquity*, xvi, 1–18; R. B. K. Stevenson in *Journ. Roy. Soc. Ant. Ireland*, lxxxvi, 84–96.

[3] F. M. Stenton, *Anglo-Saxon England*, 355 and 412; *R. Comm. Hist. Mons.: Westmorland*, l–liii.

[4] *Y Cymmrodor*, ix, 172–3.

[5] *AC = Annales Cambriae*, preserved in the same MS. as the Genealogies; *AU = Annals of Ulster*, a late medieval MS. incorporating much early material (ed., Hennessey). The reference is to the year in the printed version; these in some cases involve errors, but only of a very few years.

710–740 son of Teudubr	Teudubr son of Beli dies (*AC*: 750).
680–710 son of Beli	Beli son of Elfin dies (*AC*: 722).
650–680 son of Elfin	
620–650 son of Eugein	
590–620 son of Beli	Beli dies (*AC*: 627).
560–590 son of Neithon	
530–560 son of Guipno (for Gwyddno)	
500–530 son of Dumnagual hen	
470–500 son of Cinuit	
440–470 son of Ceretic Guletic	Coirthech rex Aloo (Ailcluaith), a contemporary of St. Patrick (*ob. c.* 460).

Another branch of the same dynasty is recorded in the following genealogy:

Floruit *Harley* 3857, *pedigree vi*	*Annalistic references*
590–620 Riderch hen	Rhydderch ap Tudwal a contemporary of St. Columba (*ob.* 597) and St. Kentigern (*ob. c.* 600).
560–590 son of Tutagual	
530–560 son of Clinoch	
500–530 son of Dumnagual hen	

Strathclyde was the only British kingdom in the north that was able to preserve its independence in the face of the Northumbrian advance into southern Scotland in the seventh-century. Previously there had been a number of other dynasties; some of their genealogies are preserved in the same Welsh source.[1] In no case do these lines reach beyond a date in the first half of the seventh century. The most famous of these rulers— his line is not recorded in the extant genealogies—is Morgan Mwynfawr, the ruler of Eiddyn, whose fatal expedition to Catraeth is commemorated in an early Welsh poem, the Gododdin of Aneirin.[2] This poem is a lament

[1] *Y. Cymmrodor*, ix, 172–5; pedigrees iv and vii–xii. Another version of some of these genealogies is given in MS. 20 of Jesus College, Oxford, a fourteenth-century MS., using a good tradition.

[2] The main conclusions of Professor Ifor Williams's standard edition (*Canu Aneirin*, Cardiff, 1938) are summarized by Professor Kenneth Jackson in *Antiquity*, xiii, 25–34.

for the heroes who fell in battle with the heathen Angles of Deira (York-shire). 'The men went to Catraeth, vigorous their host, the pale mead was their feast and their poison, three hundred fighting in ranks, and after the shout of battle there was silence. Though they went to churches to do penance, true is the tale, death overtook them.'

A British force able to strike freely from Eiddyn, which is either Edinburgh or some site on the Pentlands represented by the modern name Cariden, to Catraeth, now Catterick in Yorkshire, belongs to a time before a deep Anglian penetration, to the period in the late sixth century, when the British kings besieged Theodric of Bernicia in his stronghold on the Northumbrian coast (p. 128). The events recorded in the epic of Aneirin must have taken place not later than about 600, when the Saxons were still confined to the south side of the modern border and east of the Pennines. The whole of southern Scotland was then British. The northern boundary of this people lay on the estuary of the Clyde. 'There is', wrote Bede, 'a very great gulf of the sea, which of old divided the people of the Britons from the Picts, penetrating from the west deeply into the land, where stands to this day the very strong city of the Britons called Alcluith (Dumbarton); to the north of which gulf the Scots coming, as we have related, made for themselves a fatherland.'[1] It is probable that Bede was thinking of the lower Clyde and Loch Long rather than the course of the Clyde proper. Dumbarton (Ail Cluaith, i.e. the rock of the Clyde) lies north of the river, but its other Celtic name Dun Breatann (i.e. the fortress Northumberland and the south shore of the Forth, but the name Manaw, representing a division of their territory, is represented today not only by of the Britons) suggests a position not far from the frontier. A memory of this frontier is perhaps preserved in the name Clach nam Breatann (the stone of the Britons) on the western side of Glen Fallach, at the head of Loch Lomond.[2] Farther east the Forth, in Bede's day, separated the lands of the Angles from those of the Picts.[3] It cannot, however, be assumed that it had also formed the northern frontier of the Britons. Manaw Gododdin is celebrated in Welsh tradition as the original home of Cunedda, who migrated from the north to found the greatest of the medieval Welsh dynasties, the house of Gwynedd.[4] The Gododdin or Votadini inhabited

---

[1] *Bedae historia ecclesiastica*, i, i.
[2] W. J. Watson, *History of the Celtic Place Names of Scotland*, 15.
[3] *Bedae historia ecclesiastica*, iv, 26.
[4] J. E. Lloyd, *History of Wales*, i, 162–71.

Slanamman on the south but by Clackmannan on the north side of the estuary.[1] The description of Fife 'from the mountain of the Britons to the mountain which is called Okhel' (the Ochils) in the life of St. Serf,[2] also suggests former British possessions north of the Forth. These hints—they are no more—that Fife once lay within the British area find their confirmation in the distribution of Pictish memorial stones (p. 149). Even less trustworthy is the semi-historical Irish tale of Pictish conquests from the Britons in Fortriu (Strathearn and Menteith) and Circinn (Angus and Mearns).[3]

There is little archaeological evidence for the extent of these late British kingdoms. Mr. Stevenson has recently identified the nucleated hill-forts as the strongholds of these rulers.[4] His study of the type site, Dalmahoy in Midlothian, names a number of other examples in the Lowlands; the list can now be extended. Among other sites may be noted the much defaced remains of early banks and ditches on the east summit of Dumbarton Rock. But, as Mr. Stevenson's pioneer study makes clear, the type is found beyond the purely British area, notably at Dunadd, the capital of the Scots of Argyll, where the dating has been confirmed by excavation, and at Dunkeld and Dundurn, which must have been Pictish at this date. This extension of the type beyond the political frontier need cause no surprise. Of all the monuments easily recognizable from surface indications, the fortification is that least adapted to indicate divisions between peoples. Military convenience or necessity must quickly have outweighed the authority which any primitive society attaches to custom and have led to the adoption of up-to-date defensive methods.

The conversion to Christianity of the Celtic peoples took place in the course of the fifth and sixth centuries. The consequent abandonment of the practice of depositing grave-goods led to the adoption throughout the whole area of Scotland of a common burial rite, extended inhumation. There is, however, one class of memorial which is specifically British and does not occur in the Irish or Pictish areas. The rough standing stones with Latin inscriptions in debased capitals or a primitive form of Insular majuscule are found in Wales, the south-west of England and southern

[1] Watson, *op. cit.*, 103–4; for the stone from which Clackmannan takes its name see *R. Comm. Hist. Mons.: Fife, Kinross and Clackmannan*, no. 612.

[2] W. F. Skene, *Chronicles of the Picts*, 416: Habitent terram Fif, a monte Britannorum usque ad montem qui dicitur Okhel.

[3] Watson, *op. cit.*, 206–7.

[4] *Proc. Soc. Ant. Scot.*, lxxxiii, 186–98.

Scotland, the lands beyond the civil province of Roman Britain that were still inhabited by Britons. The Scottish distribution covers Galloway (five examples), Dunbartonshire, Roxburghshire, Selkirkshire, Peeblesshire, and Lothian, with an outlier across the border.[1] To the evidence of these inscriptions may be added that of the small simple crosses, which find their nearest analogies in Wales and are now beginning to appear in Scotland.[2]

The northern dynasties recorded in Welsh tradition can be traced back to the late Roman period; there is evidence that their founders were recognized by the Imperial authorities. Cunedda, of the house of Manaw Gododdin (p. 140) is a grandson of Paternus, 'clad in a red robe' (Padarn pesrut).[3] This must be a symbol of authority, probably one conferred by Rome on a federate ruler. He stands on the same footing as Vortepor, the Protector, of the South Welsh house of Dyfed, who is so named on a mid-sixth-century tombstone.[4] The setting up of such states as *foederati* responsible for local defence was a part of the Roman policy of the fourth century.[5]

At an earlier date the classical writers mention a number of tribes in the British area of southern Scotland. The most comprehensive list is that given by Ptolemy.[6] The Novantae, according to this author, were settled in the south-west, in what later became Galloway. Beyond them were the Selgovae, with a number of towns, including Trimontium (Newstead on the middle Tweed). To the west of these and farther north were the Dumnonii of Strathclyde. South of these were the Votadini, whose territory included Bremenium (High Rochester in Northumberland, north of the Roman Wall); as has been seen, this tribe also occupied Lothian. The geographical position is further clarified by the statement that south of the Selgovae and the Votadini were the Brigantes, whose territory stretched from sea to sea. Durham and Cumberland were certainly Brigantian and the lands of the tribe probably included a part of Dumfriesshire in the neighbourhood of Birrens.[7] Three of these tribes figure in the Ravenna Cosmography, which, in the British section, draws exclusively on classical

[1] *DGNHAS Trans.*, III, xxxi, 175.

[2] *ibid.*, III, xxvii, 158–60, and xxxiii, 179–80, one has recently been recorded at Kilmayou, west of Dumbarton.

[3] *Y Cymmrodor*, ix, 170.

[4] V. E. Nash Williams, *Early Christian Monuments of Wales*, no. 138.

[5] cf. *A History of Northumberland*, xv, 112–16: *Arch. Aeliana*, IV, xxv, 1–52.

[6] *Ptolemaei Geographia*, II, iii, 7–10 and 16.

[7] *DGHNAS Trans.*, III, xxix, 46–65.

sources. A section enumerating the *loca* in the north of Britain includes the names Dannoni, Segloes, and Manavi, which clearly represent the Dumnonii and Selgovae of Ptolemy and Manaw of the later Celtic record (p. 140). 'Greek sources suggest that locus was the term applied by the Romans to . . . tribal or religious meeting-places; and these Scottish examples may well have been the places of lawful assembly recognized by Roman treaty or frontier regulation, perhaps in the third century when the Lowlands were patrolled rather than garrisoned.' A fourth locus, Maponi, to be identified with the Clochmabenstane or, more probably, Lochmaben, would have similarly served that part of the Brigantes settled north of Hadrian's Wall.[1]

In considering the origin of these tribes the Novantae stand apart; discussion of this unit may be deferred. The other tribes may be considered together, as the archaeological record is still too scanty to establish fine distinctions.

Southern Scotland before the Roman Conquest had a number of hill-top towns. 'They normally occupy the summits of isolated hills, comprising an area of ten or more acres, sufficient for a permanent population of several hundred families, and possess a more or less regular water-supply. Dunpender or Traprain Law is the best Scottish example.' These large hill-forts cover most of the Lowlands, with the significant exception of Galloway. There is an example on the west coast of Arran. 'North of the Forth, only the fort on Turin Hill, near Forfar, really comes up to the standards of size here adopted. The White Catertun in the same county and Burghead, near Elgin, could be brought within the requirements only by including the outworks surrounding a citadel of essentially different character.'[2] We now know that these hill-top towns were occupied on the eve of the Roman Conquest (p. 145). They represent the final extension in Britain of a native tendency to urbanization, which had started far earlier in the south. Such a tendency is dependent on social and economic developments which could easily spread from people to people and is, therefore, as in the case of imports (p. 145), ill adapted to the mapping of tribal divisions. But where, as in Scotland, it is possible to find such a phenomenon frozen at a particular moment by some external force, its distribution may be significant. The close correlation between the British areas of the post-Roman age and the spread of town-building on

[1] *Archaeologia*, xciii, 15; *DGNHAS Trans.*, III, xxxi, 35–37.
[2] V. G. Childe, *The Prehistory of Scotland*, 206–8.

the eve of the invasion indicates a community of peoples within the same area at both periods. Our knowledge of the intervening Roman period is sufficient to allow us to postulate a survival of the same native people and so to carry back the identity of the British peoples as a whole behind the Roman Conquest.

It has been necessary to base this argument on the sociological evidence, as the cultural affinities of the pre-Roman town-builders of Scotland have not yet been worked out in detail. They had an Early Iron Age Culture generally known as the Abernethy Culture, so named after a site near the estuary of the Tay.[1] Imports dating this culture include fibulae of La Tène B (Class C), ring-headed pins, and spiral finger- or toe-rings.[2] A number of the forts are bivallate or multivallate.

The fibulae should indicate a date in the third or second century B.C. Recent opinion, based on the survival of these types in strata of the first century B.C. at Maiden Castle, has tended to depress this dating. This is probably unsound. The brooches and other imported objects of this culture are consistently of La Tène B character. If these imports were really retarded we should expect to find them alongside later southern types, proper to the first century B.C., including the normal La Tène D brooch of that age. The bivallate or multivallate defences of the towns do not, in themselves, date the arrival of the culture in Scotland. They may have been adopted at a later stage in its development. Moreover allowance must by made for the possibility that the earliest settlements of this people were unfortified. This was the evolution of the All Cannings Cross Culture of Wessex, and the early palisaded enclosure at Hayhope Knowe[3] points to a similar sequence of the Iron Age Culture of southern Scotland. An original dating in the second century B.C. would seem reasonable in the light of our present knowledge, and the third century cannot be excluded.

The Abernethy Culture has never been closely defined. The type site lies beyond the Tay in Perthshire.[4] The distribution of imported objects affords no sound criterion for the spread of this culture, as the trade which they represent was not necessarily confined to a single people. All that can be said at the moment is that the hill-forts of the Lowlands, south of the Forth-Clyde isthmus, seem to represent a continuous evolution, all of which lies within the Iron Age, and that they are a specialized sociolo-

[1] ibid., 236–7.   [2] Proc. Soc. Ant. Scot., lxxxiv, 129–35.
[3] ibid., lxxxiii, 45–67.   [4] ibid., xxxiii, 13–33.

gical development, which probably indicates a common origin for the dominant element in the builders.

The multivallate fortifications found on a site such as the great hill-fort on Eildon Hill North[1] and the imports both point to the south-west of England as the source of these invaders. It is not yet possible to be more precise. The tribal name, Dumnonii, which is found both in that area and in Lowland Scotland, suggests that this tribe took part in the movement. The Dumnonii of the south-west were already established in West Cornwall in the fourth century B.C., when they figure in the account of Pytheas.[2] The name can also be traced in Ireland, where the Fir Domnann took part in the third invasion recorded in the learned Irish tradition. O'Rahilly points out that the tribes associated with this invasion do not appear in the list recorded by Ptolemy and concludes that this must therefore go back to an original based on the record of Pytheas. He further notes that learned Irish speculation dates the invasion in which the Fir Domnann took part to c. 300 B.C.[3] The computation is probably worthless, but the date should indicate the relative position in the Irish historical sequence and may well be near the truth. The connexion between the Dumnonii of the south-west and of Southern Ireland has recently received some support from the excavations at Carrigillihy, County Cork. The site is a small cliff castle of the type found in Brittany and Cornwall and has the characteristic stepped back to the stone-built rampart.[4] The Scottish invasion presumably followed that of Ireland, so that tradition may be said to afford some support to the archaeological sequence.

The problem of the Novantae is complicated by the question of the Picts of Galloway. Bede records a group of Picts 'who are called Niduarii',[5] and the name has long been identified with the river Nith, which flows by Dumfries, on the east border of Galloway. Levison has shown that the form rests on a misreading of the MSS. and that the narrative demonstrates that these Picts were inhabitants of the eastern coastlands, who could be reached by boat from Melrose, down the Tweed and across the sea.[6] Later medieval records name Picti in Galloway, and the record has been

---

[1] *R. Comm. Hist. Mons.: Roxburghshire*, no. 597.
[2] *Trans. Devonshire Association*, lxxix, 15–22.
[3] T. F. O'Rahilly, *Early Irish History and Mythology*, 16, 40, and 116.
[4] *Proc. R. Irish Acad.*, lv, 29–35.
[5] *Bedae Vita S. Cuthberti*, cap. xi.
[6] *Antiquity*, xiv, 288–9.

thought to receive confirmation from the folk memory of Kreenies or Gwassogs, who survived in the hills.[1] The latter term, the Welsh equivalent of serfs, probably gives the clue; these people were the depressed remains of the British, who had taken refuge in the uplands in the face of the successive invasions of the Angles, Norse, and Normans, which overran Galloway during the Middle Ages. Kreenie is presumably a corruption of the Irish Cruithne, a word which need mean little more than British, and such they would have been called by the partly Gaelic-speaking Norse invaders of the tenth century. Scholars writing in Latin would have translated this by the normal term Picti; it is soon after this period that we first begin to hear of Picts in Galloway.

The Novantae seem always to have stood apart from the other British tribes of the south. This is shown by the genealogy of their rulers, which alone goes back to Maximus,[2] and by the establishment of a separate bishopric covering the two modern counties less a part of the eastern border towards the Nith. Archaeologically the absence of the larger hill-forts, the hill-top towns of the pre-Roman period, has already been noted (p. 143). The outstanding Iron Age discovery in this region, the fine group of metal-work from Torrs in Kirkcudbrightshire,[3] is linked on the one side with objects from the south and east of England, on the other with Ulster. But this group stands alone. It cannot be used to discuss the kinship of the people, as such objects of luxury could travel widely. Its occurrence could perhaps be used to postulate that the British people were established here as early as the second or even the third century B.C.

The British invasions discussed in this section must have been carried out by comparatively small groups, largely composed of warriors. There is no trace of the pottery traditions of the southern English Iron Age; such wares as have been found are in the flat-rimmed tradition that dominates the eastern Scottish and northern English ceramic from the late Bronze Age to the sub-Roman period.

The Picts

The historical Picts of Alba lived on the east side of Scotland north of the Forth. The tract *de situ Albaniae*, preserved in a twelfth century MS.,

[1] Watson, *op. cit.*, 177–9.
[2] *Y Cymmrodor*, ix, 172; *DGNHAS Trans.*, III, xxvii, 88–94.
[3] *Archaeologia*, xcvi, 227–34.

includes a survey of Pictland, describing the kingdom as it was before the union with the Scots in the middle of the ninth century.[1] The survey lists seven provinces. Most of the names are still extant: Enegus cum Moerne (Angus with the Mearns), Adtheodle et Goverin (Atholl and Gowrie), Stradeern cum Menetid (Strathearn with Menteith), Fif cum Fothreve (Fife with Kinross), Marr cum Buchen (Mar with Buchan), Muref et Ros (Moray and Ross), and Cathanesia (Caithness). The *Pictish Chronicle*, a document embodying the traditions of this people, provides another and older form of the same list, in which the seven sons of Cruithne figure as eponyms of the seven divisions. The list given, rearranged to follow the same order, is: Circinn, Fochlaid, Fortrenn, Fibaid, Ce, Fidach, and Got.[2] The equations between the two lists are certain except in the cases of Ce and Fidach.

These provinces represent divisions of the Pictish people. They were ruled by hereditary chiefs, later known as mormaers, though the Irish sources more than once refer to them as kings (*righ*). When the central power was weak these local rulers must have enjoyed a large measure of independence. Moreover, it is clear that the ruling house did not always belong to the same line. The survey first quoted lists Angus as the principal part (*pars principalis*) of the kingdom, and this is borne out by the great concentration of sculptured stones belonging to the latest period of Pictish rule at Meigle in Perthshire.[3] The Anglian invasion that was so signally defeated at Nechtansmere in 685 was directed along Strathmore. This points to the centre of the kingdom being in Angus as early as the seventh century, a hypothesis not necessarily invalidated by the Irish record that the victor of Nechtansmere was Brude mac Bili, king of Fortrenn.[4] But a hundred years earlier the principal ruler, another Brude, had his seat on the shores of the Moray Firth, near Inverness.[5]

The linguistic affinities of Pictish were long a matter of dispute and the question is not yet fully resolved. As has already been noted (p. 137), the Gaelic of Scotland was introduced in the fifth century by immigrants

[1] *Chronicles of the Picts*, 136; cf. *Problem of the Picts*, 46–47.

[2] *Chronicles of the Picts*, 4.

[3] For the stones see Stewart Cruden, *The Early Christian and Pictish Monuments of Scotland* (Ministry of Works). Since Meigle lies east of the River Isla, it should form part of Angus.

[4] Nechtanesmere (Symeon of Durham, *Historia Dunelmensis Ecclesiae*, cap. ix) is to be identified at Dunnichen, three miles south-east of Forfar (*Antiquity*, xxii, 82–97).

[5] *Adamnani vita S. Columbae*, ii, 32.

from Ireland into the historical kingdom of Dalriada in Argyll. There is no sound evidence of an earlier stratum of Goidelic speech in Scotland. Brittonic was spoken north of the Forth Clyde isthmus, and the latest survey by Kenneth Jackson[1] shows that Brittonic place-name elements cover the country east of the great mountain chain of Drumalban as far north as the Black Isle and south-east Sutherland. Some of these elements, such as garden, lanerc, and aber, are common to the other Brittonic-speaking parts of Britain. One of them—pet—has a main distribution north of the Forth, with sporadic examples in Lothian and one in Ayrshire. On this and similar evidence he concludes that Pictish speech included a Brittonic element different from British and possibly more closely akin to Gaulish. With the exception of Caithness, where the evidence is complicated by the later intrusion of Norse speech (p. 134), the area north of the Forth-Clyde line covered by these place-name elements corresponds fairly closely to that of the historical Pictish kingdom; there is, however, an extension to the west coast opposite Skye.

The principal archaeological monuments attributable to the historical Picts are the sculptured stones.[2] Their classification into three main classes —symbol stones, symbol stones with crosses, and crosses—has long been accepted. The chronology is still a matter of some dispute, but a range of the three classes from the sixth or seventh century to the tenth or eleventh would be acceptable to all students. Sculptured stones of the second class, symbol stones with crosses, were certainly being erected in the eighth century, with some extension backward or forward. The earlier class, the simple symbol stones, must have been current in the seventh century and may perhaps begin before 600. One point that emerges from a survey of the stones is that monuments of Class I are relatively more common in the Pictish provinces north of the Mounth, while Class II predominates in the area south of that barrier.[3] There is not sufficient evidence to show whether this should be interpreted in terms of a diversity of tradition or whether it reflects a transfer of power, and therefore of wealth, from the northern to the southern provinces in the period between the sixth and eighth centuries. In view of the historical evidence cited above (p. 147) the second explanation would seem preferable.

[1] K. Jackson in *Problem of the Picts*, 129–60.
[2] The latest survey is by R. B. K. Stevenson in *Problem of the Picts*, 97–128: cf. *Proc. Soc. Ant. Scot.*, lxxiv, 60–115, and *Antiquity*, xvi, 1–18.
[3] *Problem of the Picts*, 32.

A very large proportion of these monuments lie in the area indicated by the linguistic evidence (p. 148), including the extension to the west coast and to Skye. There are also sculptures of this type in the far north and in Orkney and Shetland, together with scattered examples in the south and west. Those last mentioned are found in areas that were certainly not Pictish at the date of their erection. Dunadd in the seventh and eighth centuries was the capital of the Scots of Dalriada, while Edinburgh and Trusty's Hill, Anwoth, Kirkcudbrightshire, were in Anglian or, if a very high chronology is accepted, British hands. I have elsewhere[1] argued that these stones are the result of Pictish raids in the period when this people was predominant in the period after the victory of Nechtansmere (685).

The discovery of Pictish monuments in the north is a different case. Caithness is one of the seven Pictish provinces, and the older name of the Shetlands, Inse Cat, connects these islands with that province.[2] The early Norse writers record the Picts as holding the Orkneys and Shetlands at the time of their first settlements in the ninth century, and name the Pentland Firth (Pettlandsfjordr) after this people.[3] A passage in the life of St. Columba shows the sub-king of the Orkneys at the court of Brude, the Pictish high king and subject to his orders.[4]

The distribution of the symbol stones confirms the historical record, but does not carry it back beyond 600. The evidence of the place-names certainly goes back to an earlier period, but how much earlier it is not yet possible to say; it points to a stage in the Pictish expansion in the north, probably a late stage. In the Roman period (late first to fourth century A.D.) the Pictish peoples must be sought on the east coast, north of the Forth and extending beyond the Moray Firth to the Black Isle and across to the west coast and to Skye.

This deduction finds some support in Mr. Hamilton's recent report on Jarlshof, in Shetland.[5] Analysing the pre-Norse sequence of the Iron Age, he writes: 'In the third phase, probably beginning in the second or early third century, new colonists arrived from the south. These people occupied large wheel houses, which are adapted from a native tradition; at a later stage at Jarlshof, they use underground passage houses. Their

---

[1] *Antiquity*, xxvii, 237–9.
[2] Watson, *op. cit.*, 30; J. R. C. Hamilton, *Jarlshof*, 91.
[3] H. Marwick, *Orkney*, 34–35; *R. Comm. Hist. Mons.: Orkney and Shetland*, i, 7.
[4] *Adamnani vita S. Columbae*, ii, 42.
[5] Hamilton, *op. cit.*, 90–91.

pottery, though hand made, is clearly influenced by Romano-British traditions, in contrast to the earlier steatite-backed ware of Iron Age A parentage.' The wheel-house complex of Jarlshof is a hybrid with southern elements and Hamilton argues convincingly that these intrusive elements are of mainland origin. That they are Pictish is a reasonable conjecture and the passage houses, which are a form of souterrain, link them with the main Pictish area, where this type of structure was in use as early as the second century.[1]

The Picts are first named in the classical record in 297.[2] On various occasions in the fourth century they are noted, often linked with the Scots and other races, as the enemies of Rome and of the British subjects of the Empire. One of the writers, Ammianus Marcellinus, recording the events of 368, mentions the two main branches of this people, the Dicale-donii and the Verturiones.[3] The second name is philologically linked with Fortrenn, the historical Pictish kingdom in Strathearn and Menteith.[4] The Caledonii are a northern tribe named by Ptolemy; their territory extended from Argyll to the Moray Firth.[5] The Caledonii were probably the leading tribe of a confederacy, since Tacitus uses the term Caledonia for the whole country north of the Forth-Clyde isthmus.[6]

The Caledonii of Tacitus were, in some sense, Britanni, an equation which bears out the linguistic evidence already cited in connexion with the Picts (p. 148). Other classical writers are less precise. It is probable that the word is used in more than one sense, referring sometimes to a particular tribe, sometimes to a group of tribes of which the Caledonii were the leaders. The components, and therefore the extent, of this confederacy were probably fluctuating. But Roman penetration along the east coast marked by a line of forts extending to Inchtuthill, Perthshire, and beyond, points to this area as the centre of the group of peoples. The classical writers view the question from the south and give no clear indication of the northern boundary of this group, but there is nothing to contradict the suggestion that it covered the whole Pictish area up to the Moray Firth and the Black Isle, and such is, in fact, the implication of Tacitus.

[1] *Antiquity*, xxvii, 219–32.

[2] Eumenius, *Panegyric xi in Panegyrici latini*, 140 (ed. Baehrens).

[3] *Ammiani Marcellini rerum gestarum*, xxvii, 8, 5: Picti in duas gentes divisi, Dicalydones et Verturiones.

[4] K. Jackson in *Scottish Historical Review*, xxxiii, 14–18.

[5] *Ptolemaii geographiae*, II, iii, 8.   [6] *Taciti Agricola*, x.

The area between the Tay and the Moray Firth is known to have been inhabited by a number of tribes, of which the names are recorded by Ptolemy.[1] Some of these names can be interpreted as Brittonic; others do not seem to be Celtic or even Aryan. This and other evidence has led Professor Jackson to identify two linguistic elements within the Pictish amalgam, one Brittonic and akin to Gaulish rather than British, the other pre-Indo-European. Such a conclusion tells us little about the structure of the amalgam. It would be compatible with a confederacy in which the two elements were on an equality or one in which one element or the other was dominant, even though it might in origin have been numerically inferior. The name Caledonii is not demonstrably Celtic, pointing to the possibility that the dominant element in this area was aboriginal and pre-Indo-European; this could explain the long survival of archaic elements, such as the matrilinear succession in the Royal house, a non-Aryan custom recorded by Bede.[2]

The latest pre-Roman culture than can be identified in this area is of a Late Bronze Age type. The typical pottery is the flat-rimmed ware, found on sites like Old Keig and Covesea.[3] Childe originally argued that recumbent stone circles, such as Old Keig, were erected by the makers of this pottery,[4] but this view has implicitly been challenged.[5] Professor Piggott now informs me that the most recent investigations make it certain that the stone settings belong to an earlier age. The dating of the pottery is not affected by this correction and its occurrence on older sacred sites is precisely what might be expected in a people formed by the amalgamation of Brittonic-speaking new-comers with the older aboriginal inhabitants. The dating of the immigrant elements depends partly on the association of the pottery with metal types of the late Bronze Age and partly on the occurrence of related wares in datable English and Irish contexts. The most important of the Scottish sites is the Sculptor's Cave at Covesea, Moray, where the metal finds include gold ring money and two types of bronze bracelet. A date in the fifth or fourth century could be accepted. Outside Scotland the analogous wares have been found on sites like Heathery Burn, Durham, where the complex may be dated to

[1] K. Jackson in *Problem of the Picts*, 135–6.
[2] *Bedae historia ecclesiastica*, i, i.
[3] *Proc. Soc. Ant. Scot.*, lxviii, 372–93, and lxv, 177–216.
[4] V. G. Childe, *Prehistory of Scotland*, 173–6.
[5] *Proc. Soc. Ant. Scot.*, lxix, 169–214; the parallels for the Iron Age wares are cited on 195.

c. 500 B.C., and in the Late Bronze Age crannog of Ballinderry, West-meath, for which pollen analysis has suggested a date rather after 400 B.C.[1]

This is not the place to discuss in detail the range and chronology of this culture. In the present context it only needs to be noted that the evidence points to its establishment in the heart of the later Pictish area at a date that can hardly be later than 400 B.C., and that developments in the full Iron Age in Aberdeenshire and the north-east were based mainly on this Late Bronze Age tradition.[2] That this tradition, in turn, incor-porated substantial ritual elements from an even earlier native culture is also relevant to the present argument.

There is one other line of research that must be considered. The Irish literati of the ninth and later centuries use the native word Cruithne (and its compounds) as the equivalent of the Latin Picti.[3] This equation played an important role in medieval Scottish historiography, but the later development of the question is not now relevant. In Ireland the Cruithne, who are not called Picti, figure largely in the native tradition. They were vassal peoples widely dispersed in the island and their name implies that they were believed to have come from Britain.

Philologically Cruithne represents an earlier Kuriteni, which has been explained as a Goidelic borrowing of Brittonic Priteni.[4] The Greeks knew the inhabitants of Britain as Πρεττανοί, at least as early as the time of Pytheas of Marseilles. His work dates from *circa* 330 B.C., a time when the Iron Age A invasions had hardly affected more than the southern and eastern coasts of England. The word Πρεττανοί is Celtic; it must therefore apply to peoples who had reached Britain not later than the Late Bronze Age. There we have a possible context for the arrival of the Brittonic-speaking element in the amalgam that later became the historical Picts.

The tentative conclusion that can be drawn from the evidence set out is that a fusion between aboriginal non-Indo-European-speaking inhabi-tants and immigrant Brittonic-speaking Celts, akin to the Gauls, took place in north-east Scotland about the middle of the first millennium B.C., and that the Picts of the Roman and sub-Roman ages were the outcome of this fusion.

---

[1] *Proc. R. Irish Acad.*, xlvii, 6–29.
[2] Childe, *op. cit.*, 255–7.
[3] T. F. O'Rahilly, *Early Irish History and Mythology*, 342.
[4] *ibid.*, 341 and 444.

The Castle-Builders of the West and North

There is one other group that we can tentatively identify in this historical or pseudo-historical record. The Iron Age of the western Highlands and Islands and of the far north is sociologically distinguished from that of the British and Pictish areas. Rahoy, the jagged summit of a crag overlooking Loch Tencuis, Argyll, is typical of the small forts of this area, with a timber-laced rampart of stone, some 10 feet thick, enclosing a roughly circular space about 40 feet across. 'Rahoy', to quote Gordon Childe, 'was the castle of a chief. His retainers and clansmen, who did the building, must in peace-time have lived outside the walls, presumably on holdings in the arable land beside the loch.'[1] This is the norm of settlement in the north and west. The brochs of the north, considered as the enduring phenomena of a specialized form of organization, are not essentially different from the duns and castles of the western Highlands.

The occupation of these castles in the last centuries before and the earliest during our era is established.[2] The people responsible for this castle culture, which contrasts so strongly with the larger settlements of the British area in the south, was not necessarily homogeneous, though features in the construction of the castles suggest a certain degree of unity or, at least, of inspiration from a common source.

This source may perhaps be connected with Ireland and with traditions of an immigration from that island into Argyll in the age preceding the establishment of the historical Scotic dynasty in *c.* A.D. 500. One of the more vivid of these traditions is preserved in the legendary tale of the second battle of Magh Tuired, in which the Irish Builg were defeated with great slaughter by the Laginian invaders. The survivors of the Builg fled oversea and took refuge in islands outside Ireland; Arran, Islay, Man, and Rathlin are named in one version of the tale. These peoples were not necessarily Goidelic speaking. O'Rahilly terms their language Ivernic and suggests that its affinities were with Brittonic. A date in the third or second century B.C. would best accord with his interpretation of the Irish traditions. The movement in the legend is pictured dramatically as a single event, but the reality is more likely to have been concerned with small groups of which the passage must be spread over more than one generation.[3]

[1] V. G. Childe, *Scotland Before the Scots*, 88–91.
[2] V. G. Childe, *Prehistory of Scotland*, 197–206.
[3] *Proc. Preh. Soc.*, xxi, 255–6.

There are reasons for regarding this movement, so far as the west is concerned, as one into an empty land. Demetrius of Tarsus, sent there on a mission of exploration late in the first century A.D., records that many of the islands were deserted and that some bore the names of spirits and heroes,[1] a fact confirmed by the list preserved in the much later Ravenna Cosmography.[2] But conditions in the west were not reproduced in the north. There the excavations at Jarlshof and elsewhere[3] have shown no evidence of a similar hiatus in human settlement. This may account for the specialized development of the broch, which was probably conditioned by the existence in these same localities of comparatively numerous earlier inhabitants of a race different from that of the castle-builders. The evidence is not sufficient to allow us to give a name to the new-comers, but it does suggest the possibility that they were connected with the peoples known to later Irish scholars as the Builg or Firbolg, whose name has been connected philologically with the that of the Belgae.

[1] *Plutarch, de defectu oraculorum,* cap. xviii. Dessau (*Hermes,* 1911, 156–60) connects Demetrius with the Greek inscriptions found at York and dates his visit to the governorship of Agricola.

[2] *Archaeologia,* xciii, 41 : s.v. Minerve.

[3] Hamilton, *op. cit.,* 90.

Index